How to Use Your Intuition to Change Your Life

By Dr. Joy Martina

TABLE OF CONTENTS

INTRODUCTION

"The intuitive mind is a sacred gift. The rational mind is a faithful servant. We have created a society that honors the servant and has forgotten the gift." ~Einstein

Einstein had it right—at least according to *Forbes Magazine*. A global media company known for having its finger on the pulse, Forbes keeps the world informed on new developments. Best known for their coverage of business, investing, and technology, they also cover more personal topics like leadership and lifestyle. So when Forbes says, "Intuition is the highest form of intelligence," leaders in the business world pay attention.

Meanwhile, even those who've never heard of Forbes use their intuition every single day. In fact, their very lives are shaped by human intuition.

A skeptic might say, "Yeah, right. You've had one too many tarot readings. How can human intuition shape someone's life?" The answer is simple: Intuition is responsible for countless insights and innovations that have shaped the world. *Everyone's world.*

Consider this: the Myers-Briggs Personality Assessment includes Intuition as one of four primary measurements, and Obama, Zuckerberg, Einstein, and Elon Musk all scored HIGH for Intuition.

Truth is the men and women who have shaped our world have utilized their highest intelligence to great advantage. The men and women who will shape the future must do the same. I'd go so far as to say that our very survival hinges on human intuition.

We'll talk more about that in Chapter 5. For now, let's see how you can use your intuition to change your life.

INTRODUCTION TO HIGHER INTELLIGENCE

Ready to continue? I'm here to help you tap into your higher intelligence by developing your intuition. Early in my career, my expertise earned many a raised eyebrow. I grew accustomed to the amused looks. When asked for my counsel in a business setting, executives would typically ignore or dismiss my advice… if they were polite. The less polite would ridicule me outright. Later, those very same people often acted on my suggestions and, as a result, experienced big breakthroughs in their business.

It wasn't that people didn't see the value in my advice. They did. They simply couldn't relate to my use of intuition. Then, when clients began to rave about my work and I started making more money than my friends in the corporate world, people started to notice.

"Seriously? Businesses are consulting with this woman and paying her *how much*? They must be onto something…"

The "something" they were onto was more than just my intuition, it was the possibility of tapping into their own. That's what I do: teach people how to develop their intuition and, in the process, access their innate genius. To that end, I focus on helping them clear limiting beliefs so they can be their happiest selves.

You see, happiness and intuition go hand-in-hand. To feel true happiness, the kind that comes from deep inside, we need to be tuned in with who we really are. The Five Steps in this book are designed to do exactly that and to strengthen your intuition in the process.

Nowadays, when I walk into a board room or executive suite, rather than earn raised eyebrows, I earn tremendous respect. That is what having a strong intuition can earn you, too—respect from your colleagues, respect from your team, respect from your family and community. What's more, honing your intuition can earn you ever deepening self-respect as you grow into a whole new level of confidence in your abilities.

Intuition As a Form of Intelligence

We've all heard of women's intuition. What we need to talk about more often is men's intuition. Human intuition. Intuition as a form of intelligence.

In the past, "women's intuition" has been readily dismissed. We women are told to trust our intuition and yet men don't always take us seriously when we put words to what our intuition *just knows*. Fortunately, that impasse has begun to give way. The more we see the value of intuition, the more open we will be to receiving its wisdom. We'll delve into the scientific evidence for the inherent value and validity of intuition in Chapter One.

Once we accept that intuition is an intelligence function of tremendous power, several obvious questions arise:

- How do we develop our intuition?
- What role does intuition play in problem-solving?
- How do you know you can trust your intuition?
- What if my intuition is wrong?
- Is intuition as available to men as it is to women?
- Can intuition be taught in schools?
- What about rational thinking and logic?
- How do we best go about harnessing the "highest form of intelligence" for the greater good?

Before we look for answers, I have one more question. If we accept that intuition is the highest form of intelligence, wouldn't you like to know how to use it to master your world? Of course you would.

Celebrity Intuitives on the Myers-Briggs Type Indicator Test

In the pages that follow you will find a systemized approach to activate and amplify your intuition. You will discover that intuition gives you a distinct advantage in difficult situations. Develop "the gift" as Einstein called it, and you will join the many celebrities and leaders who are classified as Intuitives on the Myers-Briggs Type Indicator (MBTI). You may even find yourself standing among millions of intuitive types who have changed the world, including Franklin D. Roosevelt, Margaret Thatcher, Stephen Hawking, Elon Musk, Mark Zuckerberg, and Steve Jobs.

Each of these individuals is classified as an Intuitive on the MBTI. Their accomplishments show that intuition is more than just a "neat" aptitude; it is an essential skill when it comes to creating success in the arenas of business and politics.

NOTE: The MBTI is used by 85% of all Fortune 500 companies and 89% of the Fortune 10 companies when hiring people. The test is designed to uncover individual psychological tendencies (how a person sees the world and makes decisions for example). MBTI is based on the idea that humans have 4 primary functions: sensation, intuition, feeling, and thinking. Based on Carl Jung's theory of psychological types, the MBTI was developed in the 50s by a mother-daughter team to help women find suitable jobs after World War II.

Steve Jobs, "Intuition is the Highest Form of Intelligence"

10

I don't believe in women's intuition anymore than I believe that rational thinking is the exclusive purview of men. The only real difference between men and women when it comes to intuition is that we women have more permission to trust our intuitive sense than men do. We talk about following our intuition as off-handedly as men talk about their golf game or how their team scored over the weekend.

In fact, we women are expected to follow our inner promptings, to be led by our hearts. Men, on the other hand, are expected to "stick to the facts, Ma'am." Guys are socialized to "know the score" to "gather data" and "run the numbers." They are taught to ignore or deny that secret knowing that may defy logic but prove superior all the same. Sure, a man is allowed to "have a hunch" or "follow my gut." But most men wouldn't dare utter words such as: "I just have an intuitive sense," or qualify what they know with, "My guidance told me," or, "I asked Spirit."

Still and yet, the fact remains: men act on intuition all the time. They just don't realize they're doing so. If they do, they certainly don't announce it to the world. Or they didn't until the late Steve Jobs, founder of Apple Computer, led the way.

In 2005, Jobs single-handedly boosted the reputation of our "highest form of intelligence" in a speech at Stanford University's commencement ceremony. He told the crowd: "Don't let the noise of other's opinions drown out your own inner voice. And most important, have the courage to follow your heart and intuition. They somehow already know what you truly want to become."

This begs the BIG QUESTION: What do you truly want to become?

Intuition can be looked at from any number of perspectives. In Chapter One we will consider various definitions of intuition. We will also look at misconceptions about intuitive types and bust a few myths about our "sixth sense."

"Why?" you might ask. "Why bother defining something so… so, immaterial and elusive?" Simple. We can more readily benefit from (and capitalize on) this type of knowing if we know what it is. But before we double-down on the definition, I want to share my perspective. To do that, I'm going to set aside the question "What is intuition?" for a moment and consider what intuition *serves*.

My perspective comes from having helped tens of thousands of people around the globe—in Italy, China, Germany, the Netherlands, and the United States. I have helped them resolve past traumas, release emotional "sssshtuff" and become their Greatest, Grandest Selves. What I have seen again and again is this: we humans need to be connected to our intuition to experience true joy.

In light of this, I define intuition as *a vital connection with your truest self*. That vital connection leads to success in life, whatever "success" means to you—a great career, vibrant health, fulfilling relationship, work/life balance.

The sad truth, according to the Harris Poll Happiness Index, is that most of us are missing that vital connection.

More than Half of the US Population is Unhappy

For the first time in 10 years, Americans are less happy than ever before. According to the Harris Poll Happiness Index of 2017, only 23% of Americans describe themselves as happy. That means 67% of the population is unhappy. Think about that for a moment. This is a devastating state of affairs. And it's costing U.S. companies up to 500 billion dollars a year.

The root cause of this unhappiness is the incredible information-overload our brains have to deal with every day. We have gone from receiving around 2 million bits of information per second just 25 years ago to receiving around 11 million bits per second today. That's five times the input we received in 1993, and it's speeding up even more. Experts predict that in the next three years, we will see another quantum leap in technology equivalent in magnitude to what occurred these past ten years.

This is especially alarming given that the human brain can only focus on an estimated 126 bits of information per second. Not millions of bits, a mere 126. No wonder we feel overwhelmed, stressed out, and disconnected. Never before in the history of humanity have we been bombarded with so much information. It would be overwhelming, even if all the input was positive. Sadly, much of it is terrifying—natural disasters, mass shootings, terror attacks, economic downturns, environmental threats, political scandal. Is it any wonder depression is an epidemic?

So how do we turn the trend around? How can you begin to create happiness in your life given the avalanche of input every day? How can you avoid getting buried by technology and crushed by the fear of catastrophe?

You can learn to tune into yourself and your intuition.

Strengthening your intuition and learning to trust it is simpler than you might think. Intuition is a skill and, just like any other skill, it can be learned. This becomes obvious to most people as soon as they embrace their intuition and intentionally set out to hone it. The truth is, most people are far more intuitive than they know so their learning curve is full of exhilarating moments when they realize just how brilliant their intuition is. Take charge of your mind or someone else will.

Survival in Cataclysmic Times Demands Intuition

When you become more intuitive, everyone benefits. Integrate more of your truest, most authentic self, and you'll be happier, healthier, more peaceful, and more loving. You'll also be better equipped to handle adversity—come what may.

Frank Blaney, author at The Good Men Project, put it this way: "The most precious knowledge we will need to survive in these cataclysmic times will not come from Google, but our intuition."

We can do more than survive these unpredictable times when we embrace and actualize the power of Intuitive Intelligence. I see Intuitive Intelligence coming into vogue the way Emotional Intelligence has over the past twenty years. In leadership and organizations, from our boardrooms to our legislative floors, from our classrooms to our bedrooms, we will look to those with a high Intuitive Intelligence Quotient (IIQ) to steer us toward a more coherent future.

My intention is to do all I can to increase our collective IIQ so humanity can move beyond the cataclysm to a beautiful tomorrow.

The Driver Who Couldn't Explain Why

Formula One race car driver Juan Fangio was nearing a hairpin turn when he suddenly hit the brakes without knowing why. That afternoon, he won the Monaco Grand Prix. Were it not for his seemingly inexplicable slowdown, he would have slammed into a pile-up of crashed cars.

How could he have know there was a crash up ahead? The pile-up was around the bend where he couldn't see it! Did his intuition tell him to slam on the brakes? Professor Gerard Hodgkinson of Leeds University thinks so. "The driver couldn't explain why he felt he should stop," he said, "but the urge was much stronger than his desire to win the race."

Hodgkinson believes that human intuition derives from our ability to instantly evaluate internal and external cues without processing the information with the conscious mind. In fact, Juan Fangio wasn't even consciously aware of the cue that made him brake that day.

According to Hodgkinson: "The driver underwent forensic analysis by psychologists afterwards... he was shown a video to mentally relive the event. In hindsight, he realized that the crowd, which would have normally been cheering him on, wasn't looking at him coming up to the bend but was looking the

other way in a static, frozen way. That was the cue…
he knew something was wrong and stopped in time."

Gut Feelings, Hunches, and Intuitive Hits

Have you ever acted without thinking and, as a result,
escaped danger? Ever get a funny feeling in your gut
then immediately take action and save someone else
from harm? Or " just have a hunch" to go off your
beaten track and then bump into someone you were
thinking about that morning? Have you ever made a
snap judgment like, "That person is not to be trusted"
and realized later your intuition was spot-on? Or
perhaps you made an off-the-cuff decision to go to a
lecture and met someone who changed your life.

Intuitive experiences like this happen all the time.

A team of researchers at Leeds University Business
School has deemed intuition a real psychological
phenomenon. They postulate that our intuitive abilities
are the result of the way our brains process, store,
and retrieve information.

The way I see it, we have two fundamentally different
ways of gathering information. One way is with our
five senses. We take in our surroundings and collect
information about our experiences by what we see,
hear, feel, taste, and touch. If we rely solely on our
five senses, what we can take in is limited to data we
can collect with our eyes, ears, nose, mouth, and

kinesthetic sense. The second way we gather information involves the intuitive part of ourselves. Intuition has a much broader range of inputs available. It gathers information above and beyond what we can consciously register with our senses. What's more, intuition does more than gather information; intuition instantly synthesizes it and draws lightening-fast conclusions. In other words, intuition sees the bigger picture.

Said simply, sensing and intuition are both information-gathering functions. This relates back to the onslaught of information discussed in the introduction.

According to Bruce Lipton, the unconscious mind can process 20 million bits of information per second. The conscious mind hits its processing limit at 126 bits per second. In other words, the unconscious mind processes 160k times more data than we actually register in conscious awareness.

NOTE: These are educated guesses; science has yet to agree on the processing speed of the unconscious mind. What we can say is that, according to researchers at the University of Pennsylvania School of Medicine, the retina in the human eye transmits visual input at roughly 10 million bits per second.* Another source says the unconscious processes information on impulses that travel as fast as 100k *mph. In contrast, the conscious mind processes info. on impulses that travel a mere 100 to 150 mph.*

Hard evidence on the mind's processing speed is hard to come by. But let's conduct a little thought experiment just for the fun of it. Consider this: you have an estimated 50 trillion cells in your body, each performing trillions of functions. Now imagine trying to watch 10,000 movie screens, all at the same time. You can't even imagine it, can you? The processing power and speed of the unconscious is nearly impossible to conceive. You can tap into this superpower with the 5 simple steps I will teach you in the pages that follow.

*(EurekAlert!, University of Pennsylvania, https://www.eurekalert.org/pub_releases/2006-07/uops-prc072606.php)

Why the Conscious Mind Must Lean on Intuition

What do we do with all this information that we're being bombarded with every day? How do we decide what to take in, what to screen out, what to file for later use, what to throw away?

The processing speed of our conscious mind is so limited that our "central processor" has to lean on intuition. Without intuition, we'd have no way of tracking all the information that constantly gets shuttled into our unconscious. The sheer magnitude of information coming at us would cause us to shut down. We can't possibly absorb all those inputs with our "slow-as-it-goes" conscious mind. But our intuition can. And it does so without effort—expertly.

Fortunately, intuition is totally comfortable sorting and sifting the contents of the unconscious, and totally adept at it as well. Without intuition to do the heavy lifting, we'd be so overwhelmed with incoming information that we wouldn't be able to get out of bed in the morning.

To navigate our world, we need both our sensing ability and our intuitive ability.

Some people are more inclined to trust information that is tangible and concrete—what they can verify and understand with their five senses. If they can pick it up and touch, feel, smell, see and taste it, they know it's real. These people, sensing people I call them, usually distrust their hunches. For sensing people, the meaning is in the data. They typically don't trust their intuition.

Intuitive people trust information that's less dependent on the senses. They follow their hunches, listen to their gut. They tend to recognize an intuitive hit immediately and trust that they can act on it. In this sense, intuitive people see the bigger picture all the time.

Given the complexity of the times in which we live, the big picture is crucial. If we spend all our waking moments bogged down in the problems we're facing, we feel depressed. We'll do anything to distract ourselves from pain, and that leads to feeling disconnected. When we can see the bigger picture, it's much easier to stay calm.

From a state of calm, you can readily tap into the highest form of intelligence—your intuition.

In the pages that follow, you will learn a practical approach that is both simple and easy. The Five Steps are not sequential. They support and enhance each other. It's a systematic approach with BIG payoffs that you'll notice straightaway. Use these tools to instantly expand your heart and mind. It's the layering process of taking the steps and using your inner resources that allows you to tap into the highest form of intelligence.

Layered in with these key takeaways, I will give you some of my best inner resources including:

HAPPINESS TIPS: everyday actions and attitudes to empower your life.

BRAIN HACKS: simple techniques to instantly change your brain state and frame of mind.

POWER MOVES: physical activities and postures that shift you into higher brain states.

These basic strategies are "take charge tactics." They give you the ability to jack into your mental-emotional operating system and take command.

To begin, I want to give you a power move you can use to switch into a more relaxed state whenever you choose.

BRAIN HACK: The Switch

This is a perfect state-changer you can use anyplace and anytime. It's simple and yet very powerful. All you need is your two hands.

First, a bit of context for why you're doing this. You know that the thoughts you think have a powerful impact on the reality you create for yourself. We all have days when we wake up feeling tired, or grumpy, or whatever. Then we stub our toe, or discover the coffee machine is broken, or the car won't start, or (heaven forbid!) all three. If you've ever had that kind of morning, you know the kind of state I'm talking about. If you look back and get really honest with yourself, you'll probably see that the thoughts you were thinking during this cascade of awfulness were pretty awful, too. The quickest way to stop the downward spiral is to become aware of your thoughts, recognize where they are taking you, and do this power move to switch into a more positive state, bring energy into your body, and counter-balance stress with self-care.

That said, here's how you do The Switch. The movement is like a karate chop. Use the side of one hand and chop into the open palm of the other hand. Quick little chops, six on one hand, six on the other back and forth. Go as fast as you can, alternating between your hands while taking deep breaths. (You can find a link to a video that shows how it's done in the resource section.) You're actually syncing the left and right hemisphere of the brain by making them talk to each other. You're working on all acupressure points on the side and palm of your hands at the same time. This move, combined with deep breathing, will de-stress your entire body.

To make it even more powerful, include your auditory channel by speaking aloud. Say to yourself, "I love and accept myself" while you do the karate chop. Your words will reprogram your brain and redirect your thoughts. Now you can add one more magical command by simply accepting what is. Say, "I love and accept myself, even if I feel bad right now. AND I love and accept myself, when I now choose to feel good!"

Take a final deep breath and stop tapping. Now take a moment and feel the warmth and energy in your body.

When we accept what is and immediately make a choice to feel good, we direct our focus and attention to what we actually want. Do this every time you notice a negative cascade of thoughts and you will train your brain to be more positive, to focus on what you want rather than what you don't want. This, in turn, speeds up the rate at which you can manifest what you want.

Here's the theory behind this power move. Your conscious mind can only focus on so much; it gets pretty maxed out at doing the karate chop. It may not seem like a lot to focus on, but there are actually well over 126 tiny movements and adjustments involved in this type of coordination activity. With your conscious mind preoccupied, you get access to the unconscious. In less than a minute, you can reprogram your brain and change your state. Then you are free to go out and "seize the day."

CHAPTER ONE
STEP 1: Get Out of the Buzz

The Department of Neurology at the University of Iowa College of Medicine is in the business of studying behavioral neurology and cognitive neuroscience. They did an experiment that demonstrates the beauty of intuition, and the friendly way it functions to help us.

It was a gambling experiment using two decks of cards, both of which were rigged. One was set up to give big wins and big losses; the other was rigged to have very small gains, but also pretty small losses. There were two groups of participants. One group consisted of individuals with a damaged prefrontal cortex, the other group had normal brain function. Science tells us that the frontal lobe is the most modern and most advanced part of the brain.

Participants were shown how to play the card game, and they were asked to predict the choices that they would make, to predict the cards. Here's what the study found: in participants with normal brain function, after a certain amount of time, their unconscious would take over and they would start making snap judgments. They would essentially learn from the experiences they were having while playing the card game. Participants with damaged prefrontal cortexes never developed that anticipatory sense. They continued to choose disadvantageously.

During the experiment, researchers measured participants for Skin Conductance Responses (SCR). We call those responses gooseflesh or "hairs standing on end" in common parlance. Regardless of what you call it, what we know is this: our body always reacts first.

What does this tell us about intuition? It grows stronger when we notice what's happening. Also called *pattern recognition,* your intuition takes in what's happening, catalogs it, then uses it to anticipate what's next.

This experiment also illustrates another aspect of intuition: being tuned into the body. In Neuro-Linguistic Programming (NLP), we talk about developing *sensory acuity*, which means having the ability to use our senses to make accurate observations about ourselves and those around us. It's a life-changing tool we all need to develop— rather, we need to recover. I say recover because we all had it as children. Children have very clear sensory acuity. Think about babies. If something's not right, they'll scream. They'll let you know right away.

NOTE: Of course, we then have to then figure out what's wrong. Is it a wet diaper? Is he hungry? Tired? But the baby is very, very tuned in to its own body. Unfortunately, the way we tend to bring up kids in today's world, the way we educate them, we don't strengthen that connection between body and mind, we actually disintegrate it. We focus, as Einstein says, on the rational mind. We put our efforts there, while neglecting the body, and neglecting to train the brain. So as we recover our own innate sensory acuity, we should attend to it in our children and do all we can to preserve it.

What I find intriguing about the card experiment is that sensory acuity (awareness, in this case, of skin responses) in normal participants was accurate. They were taking in those messages, even though they weren't consciously aware of the messages being sent or received. Some took a bit longer to integrate and act on the information; others were quicker. But they all tuned in to what they needed to watch for and adjusted accordingly. The participants who did not have a fully functional frontal brain were not able to do that.

Perhaps, then, the highest form of intelligence is seated in that frontal lobe of the brain.

Intuition is a Sensitive Animal

What we've explored so far leads to an obvious conclusion: we can benefit by learning to trust our intuition. Before we get into the first step, I want to pause here just for a moment and ask you to take a deep breath.

27

What I'm about to share with you CAN change your life. It could be the single most important piece of information your slow-but-steady conscious mind has ever taken in. That's why I'm asking you to slow down and take a deep breath. I want, we want, that conscious mind of yours to pay attention and really take note.

So here it is: your intuition is a *highly sensitive animal*.

That's right. The highest form of intelligence you have, with its marvelous capacities that are infinitely more sophisticated than a supercomputer, is highly sensitive.

And… there's one more detail you should know: in general, intuition speaks in a quiet voice.

Sure, there may be times when your intuition will shout at you: GET OUT OF HERE! But for the most part, your intuition speaks in a soft whisper. We can easily override that quiet voice if we're not accustomed to listening to it. Most of us haven't been trained to listen to our intuition, and we don't make time to intentionally tune in. We bump along, hearing what we hear all the time, inwardly and outwardly. For some people, the negating, judgmental voice inside their head takes up so much bandwidth that intuition's whispers don't have a chance.

Intuition may, at times, communicate by giving you a gentle inner nudge. If you're not in touch with your body, you can easily miss that nudge. Many people walk around with so much tension in their body that a tremendous amount of their life-force goes into trying to relieve the discomfort. In an effort to ease their tension, they distract, distract, distract. They may spend a good chunk of their day self-medicating with food, caffeine, alcohol, or other addictions. That inner nudge goes entirely unnoticed.

What your "Sixth Sense" Wants You to Know

Sometimes intuition comes in the form of a flash of insight, a vision of sorts. If we're not alert, we can miss these intuitive glimpses. We see what we're accustomed to seeing—a world wherein we can't win, perhaps. Some people live in a world where they've been wronged and most of their vital energy goes into nursing a grudge or licking their wounds. Whatever our perspective, what we see is what we get. We really do create our reality with how we see and interpret our world. Meanwhile, our intuition is trying to show us a different point of view.

As if that weren't enough, many of us are so absorbed in what's happening outside us, we don't even know how to focus inwardly. Rarely, if ever, do we dip into inner silence. It's not that we aren't intuitive, we simply aren't in the habit of paying attention to our inner voice. We ignore what our "sixth sense" wants us to know.

Most people have never been trained to simply close their eyes every now and again, take a few breaths and tune into their inner world.

If we want access to the vast store of information intuition holds…
If we want to hear what that quiet inner voice is saying…
If we want to be guided by our highest intelligence, we need to get acquainted with our inner world. We do that by building rapport with our unconscious mind.

I work very closely with coaching clients on developing rapport with their unconscious. At the start, many people have to examine a mistaken belief that the unconscious mind is not to be trusted. They view it as some mysterious part of them they can't control. They fear they might say or do something "weird" if they let down their guard. They're not really sure what their unconscious is all about, and they definitely don't trust it.

Underlying this fear is an assumption that unconscious mind is not part of us. If that were the case, it would make sense not to trust it. But it's not the case. The unconscious mind is part of us—a huge part of us. And beauty and magic happens when we start to trust what it knows.

You see, the trust we give our unconscious comes back to us in the form of *clear messaging.* The voice of intuition becomes clearer and stronger in the presence of that rapport.

Lightning in My Living Room

The last thing we wanted to do was replace the roof on our house but my intuition thought otherwise…

Our existing roof was perfectly fine. No reason to make that kind of investment just because of some silly recurring dream. So I went through the process I always use to check if I'm coming from fear. I worked with my emotions and detached. But the fear was still there. Odd.

Then, one day, I pick my daughter Grace up from school and when we pull into the driveway she says, "Mom, you know you're going to die in this house."
I say, "Yeah, one day when I'm really old. I can see that."
And she says, "Yeah but there's something with a fire."
I say, "Interesting. Thank you honey. Let me ponder on that."

I was careful not to let this feed my fear, but I did make a direct request to my unconscious: give me guidance here. There was no room for ambiguity. I asked for a clear message. Then I let go of my fear, confident that intuition always has my back.

When I was packing for our next trip, I got the clear message I'd requested. A loud voice spoke in my ear: "Put everything you really value in the basement."

We would be traveling for a whole month, so that made sense. I acknowledged the voice I know so well (even though it usually whispers) and said, "Okay you know what, I'll just put all the jewelry and stuff in the basement. That seems wise."

That evening, my husband and I took some extra time to connect to our guidance in a neutral and detached way, and I asked the question: "What's important for us to know?"

Without skipping a beat, my guidance said, "You need a new roof on your house."

We said, "Okay. Why?"

The reply came, "You need to replace it with a hurricane proof roof made of metal." And then, with emphasis, "This is the very next step you need to take."

Honestly, a new roof was the last thing we wanted to throw money at right then. Our home is a considerable size and there was nothing wrong with the roof we had. We were looking at a 6-figure investment that would easily have paid for a deluxe vacation for the entire family or many other fun things. We looked at each other and shrugged. We knew, there was nothing else to do but follow this guidance.

I said, "Well, we signed up for this path. If we've learned anything, it's that the guidance we get has always been right."

Roy said, "Okay, then. Nothing to do but trust." He hired a roofing company that very week. They put a steel roof on the house while we were in Europe.

Two months later, Roy and I were away from home again, leading our Heart Manifestation Experience Weekend in Germany. As usual, my mom had come to be with Grace while we were away. The two of them had just rushed back to the house. Mom knew there was a thunderstorm on the way so she'd postponed her errands to get back before the storm hit.

The thunderstorm was fierce. The worst in well over a decade. Our two big guard dogs, Maya and Boris, were so scared they were trembling. Mom and Grace snuggled up with them on the couch to wait out the storm.

That's when it happened. Lighting struck our house.

Actually, lightning not only struck our house, it ENTERED our house. A bolt of lighting came in through the chimney and formed a fireball. The fireball stood there, blazing, filling up our living room just three feet away from my mom, our daughter, and our dogs.

The builder told us afterwards, "If we hadn't put that steel roof on the house, the place would have burned to the ground with everyone in it."

Intuition Comes Through "In a Pinch"

According to Professor Hodgkinson, "People usually experience true intuition when they are under severe time pressure or in a situation of information overload or acute danger, where conscious analysis of the situation may be difficult or impossible."

Let's talk about time pressure for a moment. Ever notice that the time it takes to do a task expands or contracts to the time available? This is especially true with creative projects.

A friend of mine who writes for Elephant Journal explained it this way:

Deadlines make it happen in my world. I'll start ten days before a deadline, play with themes, scribble notes, write several bad first drafts of the opening paragraphs, then push it onto the back burner and go about my business. Then the day comes when I open iCal in the morning and see "article due " highlighted in red. That's when I sit down and, in about 3-4 hours, bang out an article that "should" have taken me the better part of a week to get in the can.

I chuckled when she told me that, no matter how often this happens, she still worries about getting articles in on time. But it's only her conscious mind that doesn't trust. Her actions suggest that, in the bigger picture, she knows her intuition—and her skill—will come through in a pinch.

In situations of acute danger such as our flammable roof in thunderstorm territory, intuition may pull out a megaphone. And when time is up and we no longer have a choice to put something off, intuition often supplies the inspiration we need. However, true intuition isn't limited to crisis situations or the pressure cooker of time.

As Hodgkinson points out, intuition can also come to our aid when we're on information overload. In today's world, that means all the time.

Modern life pretty much puts us on permanent information overload. We need our intuition to be at-the-ready and up-and-running all day long.

POWER MOVE: Find Sanctuary Inside

This power move is the antidote to feeling overwhelmed. It is a powerful way to build rapport with your unconscious mind and get to know the incredible powerhouse that can process all those inputs at once.

This power move is about learning to shield ourselves by creating a bubble of silence and protection all around us. This gives us space to BE in the present moment and actually know what that feels like. In time, you will establish a "home base" inside yourself. Once established, you can easily return to that place of quiet calm.

What you're doing is creating a personal sanctuary. You're developing the ability to step out of the drama and into peace at any given moment. No matter how chaotic life becomes, you can find your sanctuary inside. It's your place of rest and connection. My sanctuary looks like an old English garden with tropical influences. I've put sacred healing spots, ancient mystical woods, a lake with crystal clear water, majestic power animals, and many more beautiful "features" in there, and it keeps evolving! Allow your imagination free reign when you create this special place for yourself.

I advise you to enter your sanctuary before going to sleep at night. From this tranquil place, you can easily review your day and ask for guidance. Likewise during the day; use it as an oasis of peace to dip into when you need advice, rest, or inspiration. I always "go there" when I do my healing and coaching work.

STEP 1: Get Out of the Buzz

Intuition needs a quiet mind to speak its truth. You cannot hear that wise whisper if you're distracted by what's going on around you or are feeling emotional. This step is both a state-changer and energizer that functions as a superb pattern-interrupt. This is my all-time favorite tool. I practice this step daily and have taught it to thousands of people all over the world. I even teach it to 3 year old children. Use it on dysfunctional habits. It can even help you change deeply ingrained emotional patterns.

You can use Step 1, **Get Out of the Buzz**, whenever you notice you're not in a "feel good place" and take action to shift your state. The simplest way to do this is to simply STOP. Take a deep belly breath. Listen. Breathe. Close your eyes for a few seconds. Turn your focus within and listen to your thoughts. Are they aligned with how you want to feel? Are your thoughts supportive of your heart's desires? If the answer is no, immediately reframe them so they match how you want to feel. Often just the smallest bit of conscious effort will change your state. If you still feel emotional or stuck, do a combination Power Move/Brain Hack: go into your sanctuary and do The Switch.

Find a place where you can be alone and undisturbed for a few minutes (or longer, if possible). If you're not in your home, find a bathroom or go sit in your car. Before long, you will find that you no longer care about what others think and you'll feel comfortable doing this anywhere.

Begin by noticing how strong your feeling of discomfort is on a scale from 0-10.

Take a *deep* breath in and out. Close your eyes and go into your personal sanctuary. Really see as many details as you can for at least 10 seconds, longer if you can.

Now do The Switch using the karate chop move explained earlier in this chapter. You can do this with your eyes open or closed. Name the emotional state you are feeling. No matter what is going on right now, you are going to love and accept yourself. Are you Sad? Mad? Bad? Be specific. Accept it as it is… and breathe deeply!

Continue doing your karate chop move and declare your preferred state aloud. How would you like to feel instead? Happy? Peaceful? Loved? Say it out loud. Declare it to be so.

Give this your all! Really focus your mind on the matter at hand. Say the incantation out loud. Say it like you mean it. Your voice is the voice your unconscious mind trusts most, and actually giving sound to your thoughts is far more powerful than just thinking them.

Remember to BREATHE! Conscious breathing quickly shifts our emotional and mental state and provides our body with the oxygen and life force we need.

Lastly, smile! Even if you have to fake it, your brain will receive the message it's time to cheer up.

Continue until you feel at peace and in balance again, i.e.: when your stress level is at a zero. You may not get to zero after one round of The Switch (especially if it's an old trigger) but you will certainly notice a positive shift using just this simple tool. You'll be able to go even deeper with the other resources in this book. (And, remember there is an online resource guide with videos and more information. The link is at the end of the book.)

HAPPINESS TIP #1: Take a Brisk Walk

Take a brisk walk! Twenty minutes is ideal. If you're not accustomed to exercise, start out with ten minutes. Push yourself to the point where you're breathing hard. Your heart and brain will love it. As you get stronger, alternate between bursts of fast walking for two minutes, then two minutes of slow walking to recover. This simple technique has been shown to be very effective in treating depression. In one study on depression, 83% of the patients who did this for 3 weeks showed considerable improvement and all reported how delighted they were with the side effects of being leaner and fitter.

HAPPINESS TIP #2: Take a Power Nap

Take a power nap! Again, even taking just a few minutes to yourself gets you out of the buzz, but 20 minutes is ideal. Your intuition will tell you when you need to skip the walk and just get horizontal for a spell. Lay down and turn on some music. Close your eyes! Tune out of the visual overload and allow your brain to rest. Be sure the lyrics support your goals. (The last thing you need are lonely-heart lyrics that drag you down.)

Create playlists of uplifting music. One of my personal favorites to meditate with is the Devi prayer by Craig Preuss and Ananda. You can find it on their album, *Sacred Chants of Devi* or by searching "Devi Prayer, Hymn to the Divine Mother" on YouTube. I also recommend brain entrainment music, which incorporates specific brain training at a barely audible level to assist your unconscious to absorb the empowering messages you have selected. We have many suitable tracks available as free downloads on our various platforms including our two most popular programs: Sleep Your Fat Away and the Ultimate

Habits. Both include specific sleep programs to support you in manifesting your heart's desires.

CHAPTER TWO
STEP 2: Learn to Say "No" Gracefully

Ever go for a bike ride and suddenly "just know" how to jumpstart a big project that's been stalled out for days? Or stumble on the solution to a vexing problem while strolling down the beach? Have you ever had an epiphany while taking a shower?

You're not alone. In fact, you're in very good company. According to a study by cognitive scientist Scott Barry Kaufman, 72% of us get our creative ideas in the shower. In Kaufman's multi-national study, nearly three-quarters of the people surveyed reported being more creatively inspired in the shower than they are at work. "The relaxing, solitary, and non-judgmental shower environment may afford creative thinking by allowing the mind to wander freely," says Kaufman.

"Okay…" you might say. "What's your point? I can't stay in the shower all day. I have to go to work eventually."

Of course you do. That's why you are going to love the simple skill you'll learn in this chapter. It will allow you to have more of those creative moments without spending more time in the shower.

Optimize your Amazing Mind with "Strategic Slacking"

"Your best insights come in the shower for a reason—
your brain is wired
for that to happen." Brigid Schulte

Once you begin to use this simple skill, you won't have to chase after "Ah-ha!" moments. You won't have to wait until you can jump in the shower or take a beachwalk for creative inspiration. More and more, your thoughts will "just click." You'll know what to do in a sticky situation. You'll know the answer to a work dilemma. You'll see potential problems before they even start. And you'll take decisive action. You may even find yourself with more time on your hands to take that stroll down the sand.

"We want to be the best and we want to be hardworking, and I'm all for that," says Brigid Schulte, author of *Overwhelmed: How to Work, Love, and Play When No One Has the Time.* "I'm not for us all becoming slackers, although strategic slacking is very important because it allows mind wandering, which is where you're going to get your best insights."

Our *innate faculty* for mind-wandering is just one of many intuitive forms of information-processing. When we trust those innate faculties to run smoothly, our intuition gets stronger and we're on an upward spiral. Creative problem-solving starts to happen on the fly.

Your intuition will serve up the insights you need at the perfect moment. Solutions will simply arrive. No more pulling out the whiteboard to strategize a solution. That doesn't mean you'll get rid of that whiteboard. It means strategy sessions will be more productive and a whole lot more fun.

"Yes" Can be a Slippery Slope

In order to really master **Step 1, Get Out of the Buzz** on a regular basis, you will need to start saying "No" more often. I know from decades of coaching that the (as I consider life saving) task of taking 20 minutes of "Me-Time" every day to reboot can be a huge challenge for those, who are accustomed to taking care of everyone else's needs before they even consider their own.

Saying "No" can feel scary and confrontational. You want to say "Yes" to everything. People count on you to be a yes-person. You might even aspire to follow in the footsteps of Shonda Rhimes, whose hit medical drama, Grey's Anatomy, is counted among the longest-running TV shows in history. Arguably one of the most successful writers of all time, Rhimes is responsible for some 70 hours of television per season. She is one of Hollywood's most influential icons and one of the "100 People Who Help Shape the World" in 2007 according to *TIME Magazine.*

In her New York Times Bestseller, *Year of YES: How to Dance It Out, Stand in the Sun, and Be Your Own Person,* Rhimes tells the story of how she went from saying "No" all the time to stepping into her greatness by learning to take risks and say "Yes!"

Rhimes' story rings true on many levels. But "yes" is a slippery slope for many of us. If you're like me, you may need to develop the ability to say "No" before you embark on a year of "Yes!"

There's a difference between a "Yes!" with an exclamation point and a habitual "Yes" that is typical of *sheeple*, i.e.: people whose herd mentality leads them to spend millions on the latest Pokemon craze or fidget spinner fad. Another place we see this mentality is in the fashion world. Huge herds convene on websites to buy expensive designer items at 10x the original sale price, often selling out within the first 15 seconds!

This happens in the larger context of life as well. People don't question whether what they're doing is aligned with their purpose, their mission, their heart's desire—they just do what they're "supposed" to be doing or what someone supposedly "in the know" proclaims a "must-have."

"People Pleasing" Bent my World Completely Out of Shape

Most of us have been conditioned to believe that we need to please others before we're allowed to please ourselves. This is especially true for girls and women, although most men have been instilled with this belief to one degree or another as well.

Cultural conditioning reinforces odd notions in our brains: it's better to give than receive… It's better to blend in than to stand out…or else! And that finger-wagging "or else!" translates into many different perceived threats which translate into a swirl of irrational fears. We fear being judged by others. If we don't give someone else what they need, we may be abandoned, ridiculed, shamed, guilt tripped, called selfish etc. If we don't jump through our bosses hoops, we may get fired or not promoted. If we don't look a certain way, say the right things, wear certain clothes (the list goes on and on), we may not be accepted or even get rejected. We fear we won't be liked if we say what we really mean. In our closest relationships, we often relinquish our real wants and needs to meet the wants and needs of the other person so as not to risk losing their love.

Meanwhile, your very DNA mandates that you maintain relationships with the important people in your world no matter what. Humans are tribal by nature, after all. We can't actually "go it alone." We need our "tribe" to survive. We rank the needs and wants of others above our own. We make what's going on out there with other people the priority and brush aside what's going on inside. We essentially tell our inner selves, our intuitive side, "I don't care about what you say. I need them to love and approve of me… that's all that counts."

I'm exaggerating to make a point here, but only a little bit. In reality, for many of us, this "better to give than receive" notion becomes a mandate that operates below the threshold of thought. It's a subtle mind game we play with ourselves. Subtle, but often all-pervasive because it turns into a habitual way of being.

In my case, the habit of "people pleasing" bent my world completely out of shape.

The Cost of Over-Giving

The way I was brought up, "people pleasing" was just what you did to get along with people, to keep the peace. You're nice, you do everything for others, and then they'll like you, right? Like so many women, I was conditioned to please.

When our focus is on pleasing others in order to be okay, we neglect our own desires and needs. Often we end up feeling frustrated and underappreciated.

We start to begrudge those we're trying so hard to please. But we are the ones putting on the pressure, not the people we begrudge. That took me awhile to figure out.

I was bumping along, being nice to everyone, doing what I always do to get by: ignore my own needs and power through. Then one day I overheard my mother-in-law on the phone with my sister-in-law. I had come home early that evening. What I heard shocked me deeply. My mother-in-law was shredding me to bits, calling me the most egotistical person she knew, a lousy mother and wife. She faulted me for pursuing my education, for having interests beyond my role as a mom and traditional housewife. She spoke as if I were a criminal because I delegated the task of ironing my husband's shirts to someone else. She launched this tirade while babysitting my 9-month old son. I was horrified and hurt beyond measure. My whole, elaborate "be the perfect wife, mother, and daughter-in-law" strategy had failed. All of that effort and I was being judged behind my back. Harshly. The worst part was that I hadn't even noticed how much resentment and judgment was going on while these two women were being sweet as sugar to my face. I felt betrayed.

So why was I going to such lengths to try to please these two women? Or anyone else for that matter?

That was a turning point. Their blatant inauthenticity showed me how inauthentic I had been by trying to please people. I was neglecting my truth by rarely speaking up and constantly giving others what I thought they needed, even though it often went against my own desires. I realized that my "I'm just being a good person" act was a sham, a lie. The only person I was deceiving and betraying was myself. Even more alarming, I saw that this pattern was pervasive in my life.

I had to get real. So I asked myself, "What am I trying to prove?" When I got really honest, I had to admit that the primary motivation behind my constant efforts to please everybody was to get love as well as to safeguard myself because, truth be told, I was terrified of being rejected, excluded or not approved of.

It was one of those "once you wake up you can't go back to sleep" situations. Once I saw the inauthenticity of doing for others to gain their approval, that old way of giving became incredibly painful. I would get myself into a situation where I'd give and give and give, push myself aside, ignore my own needs and intuition, and give some more. I'd get home in the evening feeling absolutely drained. I'd look back on the day, and realize, "This cannot be what I came for, this isn't real love. I must be missing something."

Then I started to notice the difference between that old way of giving and *true giving*, giving from love, without any attachment. It was crystal clear: when I'm truly coming from love, doing for someone simply because I want to, the benefit to the receiver is far greater than when my motivation is to gain their approval. And I feel energized and fulfilled instead of drained and frustrated. Giving simply doesn't carry the energy of love when motivated by a need to please or to get something back.

Metaphorically speaking, true giving is like feeding someone a nutrient-dense meal of colorful organic fruits and vegetables with healthy proteins and good fats prepared with great love. The pleasure you see on the other person's face, when they enjoy your gift, fills you with joy. Giving to get acceptance is like feeding them a heartlessly prepared meal of tasteless, nutrient-free processed food and demanding praise.

The Gift that Keeps on Giving

We all know what true giving feels like—those times when you give with a joyful singing heart. Sometimes called random acts of kindness, they feed the soul even when the task is difficult. There's no "trying to prove something" involved. You feel love in the doing. You're not acting out of a need to get love, you're acting because *you are love.*

When we over-give, the downstream effect is often worse than the immediate impact that a "no" would have on the relationship. If the pattern is pervasive in most of our relationships, we can suffer what I call the "empty vessel syndrome." Said simply, you give so much you have nothing left to give.

In contrast, when I take care of myself and make sure my vessel is full, I am the gift that keeps on giving. The more I give, the more I get - automatically.

When we give from a place of fullness, the giving feels good. It's important to make filling up a priority and establish a baseline that gives you that powerful, safe foundation for your most radiant, confident self. With that as your starting point, you will have much more to share. And the giving feels better for everyone involved.

Have you ever been on the receiving end of the give-to-get equation? Ever have someone do something for you, go that extra mile, not because they wanted to, but because they wanted to please you or to get something back from you for it? Do you remember how this felt sort of "sticky"?

Likely you knew at a gut level their heart was not in it. It happens all the time. We all do it. We all know when someone's giving is inauthentic. We "just know." That's our intuitive power. We know when it's not real.

What would happen if we all became a little more real? That's the aim of Step Two. Before we can truly learn to say "No" gracefully, we need to get honest with ourselves at an even deeper level. We need to look at what we've been conditioned to do when someone tells us "No."

Masters of Manipulation

We learn to avoid confrontation very early in life. It's easier just to please others rather than speak our truth and express our desires. Unfortunately, when we fail to speak up and ask for what we want directly, our desires tend to side-wind, and we begin to manipulate to get what we want.

This tracks back to when we were kids. From age 0 to 7, children are in a very open brainwave state. It's the stage of life where we're getting programmed on how to behave as humans. Evolution designed us to learn what's expected of us so we can get along with "our kind." We watch to see what the "big people" do as well as how our peers behave. Then we copy that behavior. In today's world, that typically involves four ways to manipulate.

It's a curious paradox. We are essentially "trained" at a young age that we have to manipulate to get what we want. Odd, then, that once we reach adulthood we're so quick to judge others (sometimes quite harshly) for being manipulative. In reality, we all manipulate in one way or another! Some of us are more aware of it than others, of course. Some of us have learned to be direct rather than default to unconscious maneuvers to get what we want. Most of us have manipulative tendencies that pop up on occasion.

Let's look at the four basic ways we manipulate. We go about getting what we want by:

1) Being nice and trying to please.
2) Being nasty and creating a disruption, for example: going on attack or throwing a tantrum.
3) Being stubborn and digging our heels in, which can involve outright refusal to cooperate.
4) Taking on a victim role.

Let's see how this plays out between a mother and her child in the supermarket.

A mom and her daughter (we'll call her Tina) walk up to the checkout line with a basket full of groceries. As usual, the racks on either side of the line are loaded with all kinds of sweets. Let imagine that Tina's favorite strategy is #1 above. She says, "Oh Mommy, you are the best mom in the whole world. I love you so much! Can I have some candy?"

Let's just presume her mom says no. Tina might very well go on to the next strategy and throw a tantrum right there in the store. Or she might get nasty toward her mother and say, "I hate you! You're so mean!"

Mom still says no.

They get home from the grocery store and Mom starts to unpack the groceries. Tina storms to her room saying, "I'm never going to talk to you again." Mom ignores her tantrum.

An hour later, Mom knocks on her bedroom door and says, "Wash your hands, dinner will be ready in 10 minutes."

Tina says, "I'm not coming out until I get my candy."

Mom doesn't budge. "Okay, then. That's your choice. Just stay in your room." Stubborn refusal isn't working either.

Tina stews in her room for ten minutes then starts feeling helpless about getting what she wants. She walks up to Mom and says, "You're always so much nicer to my brother. Why don't you love me? He always gets what he wants. I never get anything." Tina has resorted to strategy #4, victim mode.

If we're honest with ourselves, we will have to admit that we've used all four strategies at some point in our lives. It's how we've been conditioned. It's a learned behavior. Which means it can be unlearned.

Once you start to see these patterns in yourself, you have a choice. You can pause and ask yourself: "Do I really need to do this? Is my need so important right now that I need to manipulate to get it? Or is there a better way of getting my needs met?"

The answer is yes, there is a better way. We can take an agile approach to getting our needs met; we just need the right tool so we can make a power move. That's where empowering questions come into play.

BRAIN HACK: Ask Empowering Questions

You might have noticed that the mind tends to focus on the what's not right or doesn't work. When we zoom in on what's not working, our vision gets so narrow we can't see what is working. Sound familiar?

For the longest time, the primary question that was running my life was, "What the F is wrong with me?" I would ask myself that question all the time. I was convinced that if something was not going right it was because I was doing something wrong or, worse, there must be something wrong with me. I have always had a keen eye for detail and prided myself on being able to identify mistakes or areas that could be improved. My experience of life was that it was happening to me rather than for me. At some point I became painfully aware of this and intentionally started to switch my focus. I started asking myself empowering questions, *especially* when things were not going right (i.e. the way I had planned them).

Here's how that plays out. Let's say I miss my plane. The old me would say, "Oh, what the F is wrong with me? Why can't I get it together? This is the worst thing that could happen!" Nowadays, in a situation like that, the new me asks, "How is this a blessing? Why is this the best thing that could happen to me right now?"

When we ask that kind of empowered question, we flip a switch in our brain and something fun happens. Our unconscious mind starts coming up with strategies. It comes up with answers. Because that's how our brain works. You ask good questions, you'll get great answers.

Sample Questions to Empower Your Intuition

Below is a short list of empowering questions to give you a feel for what I mean. You will find it easy to add more of your own. Next time you're in a pinch, ask yourself questions like these:

What's good about this situation?
How can I turn this into a blessing?
What am I learning right now?
What's my intuition telling me?
What is the most loving thing I could do for myself right now?

Next time you find yourself focusing on what's gone wrong, ask yourself empowering questions. Make it a habit to ask at least three empowering questions throughout the day. My favorite is: "How can I experience even more grace now?"

Remember: the mind that created the problem is not the mind that's going to solve it. When we ask empowering questions, we get answers from our intuition that will take us places we couldn't possibly get to with our conscious mind.

Make Joy Your Baseline

We always share our joy—when we have it to share. But if you're not looking after yourself, not taking time for yourself, if you allow yourself to get really stressed out, what do you have to share? You may give of your time, but you will end up sharing your stress and frustration as well. If you over-give, you'll likely start feeling resentful at some point, which means you'll also be sharing your resentment.

The only one who can dial back the tendency to over-give is you. The only one who can carve out time for self-care is you. The only one who can stake a claim on your mental, emotional, and spiritual wellbeing is you. When you stake that claim, you can find the inner spring that is your natural joy.

Surely, you've felt that natural joy at some point in your life. You've probably been there for periods of time. You recognize that self-loving, "I'm worth it" feeling. Then you get swept up into the stream of life. Other people's needs start bearing down on you. You buy into the fear you might lose their esteem if you take care of your own needs. Next thing you know, you've lost touch with that natural joy.

That's why I encourage you to do whatever it takes to establish an "I'm worth it" baseline of stable joy. You really can live in a consistent state of fullness that sustains you and, in turn, is uplifting to others. If a champion people-pleaser like me can do it, so can you. Find that baseline and tap into an infinite flow of joy that uplifts every part of your life.

How? By developing a simple skill: the ability to say "No" with grace.

Step 2: Learn to Say "No" Gracefully

It's true what they say: "No" is a complete sentence. It's also true that saying "No, thank you," with genuine kindness is much easier for others to hear. What's more, when you can say "No, thank you" with an inner smile that whispers, "I'm honoring myself in this moment," you give yourself the gift of self-respect. It also reinforces your commitment to carving out more time for relaxation and play.

However, in the pressure-cooker of work, family, romantic relationships, civic obligations and the like, it's easy to default to "Yes" without thinking. That's why I highly recommend you practice your gracious "No." Rehearse in front of a mirror. Below are some practice lines. Play around with these phrases; customize them to your individual style. If you get a lot of requests via email, write your favorite gracious "No" on a post-it note with a smiley face and put it on your computer screen.

This list is just a beginning. As you start feeling the power of saying "No" graciously you will find yourself adding to the list.

"No, thank you."
"Thank you but I have to say no."
"Thank you, I'm going to pass."
"What a lovely offer. I appreciate you thinking of me but I have to say no."
"I wish I could help. I have a prior commitment so I have to say no."
"I am sorry, that won't work for me. Is there another way I can help?"

HAPPINESS TIP #3: If it's Not a "Hell Yes!" it's a "Hell No!".

I have a playful mantra that comes in quite handy at moments of choice. I invite you to try it out for yourself. Use it as an internal gauge when you have to make a yes-or-no decision. This mantra will eliminate a lot of those messy maybes. I suggest you give it a whirl next time you're out shopping just to see how it feels.

Here's the mantra: If it's not a "Hell Yes!" it's a "Hell No." (Imagine what your closet would look like if you ask that question every time you go shopping!)

What would your life look like if you made every important decision by breaking it down to this simple rule? How often would you say "No" sooner and thus save yourself the time and energy that goes into waffling over a decision? How often do you have to go back and retract a "Yes" that would have been a "No" if you'd applied this rule? Can you see how this would give your "Yes" more impact?

We often over-complicate our decision-making processes by getting stuck in our heads and over-analyzing all the pros and cons. Meanwhile, our intuition generally knows right from the start if it's a "Hell Yes!" or a "Hell No!"

I'm not suggesting you go around saying "Hell Yes" all the time. I am suggesting you train yourself to become a decisive, high-impact "Yes!" person, who makes wise choices coming from your highest intelligence. When you can say "Yes" with the energy and emotion of a "Hell Yes!", you put yourself in a powerful position. You also give yourself a huge boost when it comes to understanding and applying the laws of manifestation. Think about it. The more energy you put out with the level of clarity, energy, and intention contained in a "Hell Yes!", the bigger the ripple effect in the Universe and the greater the reward. You can read more on this topic of The Universal Laws of Manifestation in our book "The Little Book of Karma".

To sum up this chapter, once you develop the simple skill of being able to say "No" with grace, you will experience surprising benefits. Most notably, you get a nice uptick in bandwidth that will give your intuition room to grow.

CHAPTER THREE
Step 3: Forgive & Release Joyfully

Before we talk about the third step to strengthen your intuition, let's talk about emotions. Human emotions have survival value. They contain vital information we can use to our advantage. We mustn't ignore or misunderstand that information. The consequences of ignoring our emotions is beyond the scope of this book. For the purpose of our discussion here, I want to zoom in on how we often misunderstand the vital information our emotions convey.

Your emotions influence nearly every decision you make. They have a powerful impact on your relationships, your career, your physical and mental health, the success or failure of your every endeavor. It could even be said that your emotions establish your direction in life.

Given the huge role emotions play in our lives, it's odd that we were taught so little about how to deal with them growing up. Most of us have had to figure it out for ourselves. Unfortunately, we often have to figure it out while in the midst of an emotional storm. No surprise, then, that a lot of us feel baffled when powerful emotions buffet us around.

The net effect is that most people—even smart, successful people—tend to fumble on occasion when dealing with strong feelings.

A Precious Natural Resource | Energy in Motion

Feelings. We all have them, we all revel in them when they're the "feel good" type, and we all suffer when bad feelings overtake us. But exactly what are these waves of feeling?

The word emotion derives from the French word *émouvoir* (excite) based on Latin *ēmoveō* (to move out, stir up, agitate). It has often been said that emotions are (E)motion, i.e.: energy in motion. This may seem like an oversimplification at first. But that simple statement can deliver a crucial insight that has the power to set you free.

I consider emotions—that "energy in motion" you experience as your feelings—a precious natural resource. It can be directed outwardly toward other people and all sorts of activities, or it can be directed inwardly to light up our inner world.

Emotional energy brings individuals and groups together; it is the glue that bonds us to friends and family, to our communities, our pets, all the things we love. Emotional energy fuels our life purpose and allows us to face and overcome obstacles and challenges.

63

We put our emotional energy to good use in myriad ways every single day:

- to fuel our dreams and goals
- to power our relationships
- to keep our loved ones feeling safe
- to maintain a sense of warmth and cooperation with those around us

Emotions build bridges between people. They can also erect walls that separate us.

Unresolved emotions keep us stuck. Most of us carry the burden of unresolved anger and grudges that weigh us down to one degree or another. Dropping that burden is the aim of **Step 3, Forgive and Release Joyfully.**

Let's discover how you can forgive and release joyfully to strengthen your intuition. We will look at how you can turn your emotional energy into a renewable resource and, in turn, change your life for the better.

Rocket Fuel for Personal Growth

If emotions are energy in motion, what happens when the mind tries to stop the motion?

What about those situations when the motion steers us in the wrong direction?

Ever get the feeling you're heading down a blind alley, but find it impossible to turn around?

Would you like to have an inner GPS that signals you when you need to course-correct before you waste your time and energy?

Why does the energy go round and round in a circular motion at times? We all know that "chasing your own tail" feeling, that state of confusion when we're "going nowhere fast."

And what to do about strong feelings that drive us in a backward motion, or cause us to regress and throw a temper tantrum?

These are common sticking points. **Step 3, Forgive and Release Joyfully**, will bring your feelings, and the powerful "energy in motion" they contain, into a symbiotic relationship with your intuition. Emotions are like weather patterns; they come and they go. When we allow our emotions to come and go, to move in their natural pattern, our energy flows freely. We can readily see this in very young children, in how readily their emotional states change.

Most of us were taught to suppress the free-flow of emotions. The messages came at us from all directions: "Don't be a baby… Be a big girl… Boys don't cry… Don't be sad… Good girls aren't angry." Once we enter adulthood, the suppression continues: "Emotions have no place in the workplace… Don't be so emotional… Keep your feelings to yourself… Pull yourself together and be professional…"

We all know the score. But do we know the cost?

The truth is, when we tamp down our emotions to fit into the emotionally repressed world around us, we also tamp down our aliveness. We become less than fully authentic with others and less than fully authentic with ourselves. We lose touch with our heart's desires (more on that in the next chapter). The net effect is often loneliness, isolation, even alienation—all of which can lead to depression.

Now, I'm not suggesting you should let it rip and express all your feelings all the time. We don't want to go to the other extreme of "high drama." Too much feeling can cause those around you to tune you out. When we can allow emotions to be what they are— energy in motion—we can harness that energy for the greater good. When emotional energy is truly understood and used effectively, it can become rocket fuel for personal growth and transformation.

Emotional Expansion and Contraction

What we call an emotion is really the experience of a feeling, a current of energy moving through the body. That energy has a specific quality. We will feel tense or expansive, excited or relaxed, agitated or calm. At the most basic level, our feelings impact our physiology. We literally expand or contract in response to feelings.

These currents of energy have a lifespan of a few seconds to a few minutes. When we hold onto them, their lifespan can extend for hours, even days. If we become identified with a certain feeling state, they can last for weeks, even decades.

Negative emotion causes the muscles to tense up, the skeleton to collapse, the posture to slump forward. We tend to withdraw from unwanted experiences. In contrast, positive emotion causes muscles to relax. Your posture opens up as you expand out into the room and move toward or with a positive experience. Think of a sprinter crossing a finish line, arms extended overhead in triumph. Or that feeling of "Yes!" that opens your chest when you've tackled a vexing problem. Or when your arms spread wide with excitement to welcome someone you love as they step off the plane.

My husband, Dr. Roy Martina (MD) writes about this in his international bestseller, *Emotional Balance.* He shows how unresolved emotions create stress patterns in the body and brain. These stress patterns are often at the root of stress, disease, and self-sabotaging habits that disempower us. In contrast, emotional balance fosters emotional mastery. That's when feelings become a natural resource, renewable energy. This, in turn, increases emotional intelligence and supports our ability to access the highest form of intelligence. The desired uptick in IIQ becomes more and more real.

The Science of Positive Emotion

Dozens of randomized, controlled studies have shown how much better we function after even a small infusion of positive emotion. Participants in one study were shown either a happy photo (a puppy or sunset, for example) or a neutral photo (such as a chair). The individuals who were exposed to happy images were able to come up with more ideas on what to do next when presented with a problem.

In another study, test subjects who were given a gift had better problem-solving abilities. Researchers have found that when children are asked to call up a happy memory before taking a math test, they test better. Even physicians have been found to make better recommendations on a complex case after they are given a boost of good-feeling energy.

Review the literature and you will see convincing evidence that people who are induced to feel positive emotions are:

- More trusting.
- More likely to come up with win-win solutions in negotiations.
- Able to see larger systems and register interconnections more readily.
- More effective at addressing complex problems.
- More likely to look beyond racial and cultural differences.

Just as a flower opens to the sun, the human body opens to the warmth of positive emotion, thus allowing for the emotional energy to move in the direction of joy.

Positive Emotion Expands Peripheral Vision

We've seen that intuition is far better equipped to grasp the bigger picture than the conscious mind. Intuition let's you absorb a vast amount of data that the slow processor of your linear mind can't possibly take in and turn into coherent thoughts. Scientifically speaking, positive emotion literally improves our ability to see the bigger picture. And I do mean literally; the changes can be measured at the level of our physiology.

For example, positive emotion has been shown to increase the expanse of our peripheral vision. Under the influence of positivity, the visual cortex can pick up global as well as local detail. Changes in eye-tracking allow us to see more nuances in a complicated array of images. When we are feeling afraid or angry, our eyes tend to zoom in on what's front and center, but when we're feeling positive emotions, the scope of what we scan for widens. Pattern recognition also improves.

So if positive emotion makes us smarter, more resilient, more creative, better able to see and understand the complexities of life, why do we so often hold onto negative emotion? Perhaps we just don't know a better way—yet.

What I most want you to hear is this: a simple shift in perspective can make it easier to bounce back from any setback you experience. What's more, when you make this simple shift, you can achieve a state of stable joy.

All it takes is being willing to release past hurts.

The Positivity Ratio | Flourishing at 75% Positivity

Barbara Fredrickson, PhD is a Professor of Psychology at the University of North Carolina and pioneer researcher in the field of positive psychology. She puts an interesting spin on the (E)motion =

energy in motion equation: the spiral effect of emotions. Fredrickson's research demonstrates that feelings of joy and happiness put us on an upward spiral that expands as it ascends. On the other hand, feelings of resentment and fear lead to a downward spiral of contraction.

Frederickson postulates a 3:1 "tipping point" of positive to negative emotion. When 75% of our experience is what she calls *positivity,* we humans flourish. We might even start jumping for joy!

Frederickson's research mirrors the work of John Gottman who found that successful marriages have a "magic relationship ratio." According to Gottman's website: "The difference between happy and unhappy couples is the balance between positive and negative interactions during conflict. There is a very specific ratio that makes love last."

For couples, that balance is a 5:1.

Similarly, Fredrickson suggests that the delicate balance for individuals is 3:1. We do best when we have three heartfelt, positive emotions to balance out each negative emotion. That's called the *positivity ratio.*

Fredrickson points out that this ratio gives us a wide enough range to experience all the human emotions. The goal is not to eliminate negativity altogether. The

"Don't Worry, Be Happy" approach to life tends to backfire. You've likely run into the zealous Pollyanna types. These eternal rays of sunshine are often perceived as phony, insincere, even hypocritical. And they can easily fall prey to another human foible: denial of reality.

In the professional, workday world, maintaining a 3:1 balanced positivity ratio supports:

- High productivity.
- Smoother communication.
- More effective teamwork.
- Better customer and client relations.
- More flexible problem-solving.
- Creative breakthroughs.
- Increased resilience.
- Greater engagement, enjoyment, and sense of wellbeing.
- More skill when dealing with difficulty, disappointment and loss.

Bottom line: negativity narrows our focus whereas positive emotions broaden our perspective. And that broader perspective translates to higher functioning overall.

The Two Wolves Inside | Which One Will Win?

In my work with thousands of people over the years, I have seen individuals make a massive shift toward positivity by releasing the past. Like positive emotions, the power of forgiveness has been well-researched and documented.

When it comes to holding grudges, a Cherokee parable is worth a thousand statistics.

A young boy is walking down the trail kicking the dirt, obviously upset. His grandfather sees him and asks, "Why are you kicking the dirt?"

The boy starts to gripe about a friend who has done him wrong.

His grandfather interrupts him saying, "I, too, have felt great hatred at times. But hate wears you down. It's like swallowing poison and hoping your enemy will die. I have struggled with hate many times."

The boy says, "You have, Grandfather? But I've never seen you hurt anyone."

"Son, that's because I have two wolves inside me. One wolf lives by the motto 'Do No Harm.' He lives in harmony with all of life and is impossible to offend. He feels joy throughout his days. He is filled with awe much of the time. He only fights when it is right to do

73

so, and only in the right way. The other wolf is full of hate. The smallest thing can make his temper flare. He fights with everyone all the time and is always complaining. He gets offended by the smallest slight. Sometimes his anger becomes so great, he can't even think straight. But his anger doesn't change a thing."

Then the old man stopped on the trail, put his hand on the boy's shoulder and said, "It's hard sometimes, having these two wolves inside me. They often battle with each other over my spirit."

The boy looked in his grandfather's eyes and asked, "Which wolf wins, Grandfather?"

The old man replied, "The one I feed."

We all want harmony in our lives. We prefer a life filled with awe over a life full of hate and anger. So what gets in the way of forgiveness? Why do we continue to hold onto the past if it blocks our joy?

Simple: the angry wolf, like the conscious mind, can't see bigger picture. But the wise wolf can. The wise wolf can see with the eyes of forgiveness because the wise wolf understands the larger perspective. Step Three is all about that shift in focus.

Let's put this in context and see what the wise wolf knows about our basic human needs. Then we'll map that onto **Step 3: Forgive and Release Joyfully.**

Our Basic Human Needs

It goes without saying: we all have basic needs. We need air to breathe, water to drink, food to eat. We need a safe place to lay our head at night (unlike wolves who can get by on a 15-minute "wolf nap" a few times a day). Without these basics, we wouldn't survive. We have higher needs as well. The need for security and love is part of the package we are as humans. We need empathy, rest, recreation and play. We also need meaning or purpose in life. We need a way to express our creativity. And we need freedom and autonomy.

It's easy to accept that we all have these basic needs. Clearly, some of us are doing a better job of getting those needs met than others. Regardless of whether we know how to get what we need or not, we continue to try. It's just what we do. That's why these needs are referred to as "existential" or "ontological." They're intrinsic to what it means to be a human being.

For the purpose of discussion, let's accept that every single one of us is just trying to get our needs met. And let's acknowledge that having an unmet need creates discomfort. That said, it's obvious that we humans sometimes go about getting our needs met in unskilled, even clumsy ways. We get stuck in old patterns. We think we can only get a need met in a certain way. Our efforts may be at cross-currents with another person's needs. Sometimes the cross-currents are mere ripples that come and go with the breeze. Other times they become huge waves of emotional disturbance.

What's more, we're prone to telling ourselves stories to explain why we feel what we feel. Unfortunately, it is often the meaning we give our emotions and that story we tell ourselves that creates the pain. Often, the moment we let go of the meaning we've assigned to what someone said or did is the moment we are free to feel our natural joy again.

When you hear malintent in someone's words, you are caught in the illusion that you can be hurt by their words. If you let go of that, you can detach and notice the feelings rather than be run by the emotions.

How Small Ripples Become Waves

When we default to a negative story (i.e. "get triggered"), what's actually happening is that our unconscious maps the current situation onto a similar situation from the past. This happens in a fraction of a second. Bam! Our unconscious is back in the past when something similar was said or done and we made it mean something. Along with the meaning comes the emotional disturbance. This is how small ripples become huge waves, even riptides that carry us far away from someone we once loved.

If you can accept that we're all just trying to get our needs met, you change the frame around the person whose words triggered, hurt or angered in you. If you can see that person as someone who is just trying to get their needs met, that shift in perspective opens the heart. An open heart is what you need to practice the art of joyful forgiveness.

Maybe the person you're angry with didn't know a better way to go about getting what they need. Maybe the way they went about it was outright wrong. But maybe, just maybe, there wasn't a shred of malintent involved. And here's the really beautiful part: maybe, just maybe, you don't have to take what they said or did so personally. Maybe you weren't their "victim" or even their "opponent." Maybe that person was just dealing with their stuff and you happened to be on the other end of it. And maybe you were on the other end of it because you wanted to learn something.

Let's do a little experiment. Think about a circumstance where you experienced anger, hurt, or resentment. Now look at the situation with this bigger-picture perspective in mind. Detach from the emotional content and simply adopt a new point of view. Ask yourself: "Is it possible they were just trying to get their needs met? Could it be that they were doing the best they could with the resources they have?"

POWER MOVE: Detach from "The Story"

When you get triggered, step back from whatever story you're telling yourself and say to yourself: "How interesting! I wonder where that's coming from?"

Stop. Listen. Breathe. Ask yourself: "Have I felt like this before? What does it remind me of? What am I making this mean? And is that really true?"

Breathe again. Check in again. If you still feel triggered, do The Switch. Can you release the emotions and change your perspective? In doing so, you take your power back from the negative story and release whatever has been triggered from your past.

You can take this one step further with liver tapping, which I'll explain in detail at the end of the chapter when we get to Step Three. All you need to know for this move to be effective is that the liver is one of our biggest detox organs. Your liver is under your rib cage on the right side of your body; you can't miss it if you tap that area. Tapping the liver helps release anger and gets stagnant energy moving.

Tap your liver while saying aloud: "I'm going to release this now. I'm choosing anew. Whatever happened in the past, stays in the past. I'm taking the lesson, and I'm moving on."

Now, from this broader perspective, reflect on the impact that experience in the past had on you. Did it make you stronger and more loving? Has it contributed to who you are today? Are you a wiser person for the experience you had? (You won't always know what event in the past installed the trigger, but most often you will know right away… go with that first memory that bubbles up! Trust your Unconscious!)

When we're able to preserve the learnings from painful experiences, the practice of forgiveness becomes really easy. In fact, forgiveness and release can actually become quite joyful. Holding on to past hurts perpetuates the hurt. Holding a grudge, feeling so justified in blaming someone for hurting us, just creates more pain. And science has shown that it not only creates pain, it creates disease. Our organs, our bodies take a beating when we hold on to grudges and anger.

STEP 3: Forgive and Release Joyfully

This step will help you take control of your mind so those old stories can't hold you hostage.

I intentionally use the word release rather than "let go" because, for most people, letting go feels like it requires effort. Release, on the other hand, has a feeling of sweet surrender.

When we release, we're dealing with the liver. According to Chinese medicine and kinesiology, the liver is linked to the emotion of anger.

Start by taking a deep breath. Feel whatever you are feeling. With your right hand, start tapping the area around your liver. Your liver is a huge organ that sits underneath the whole right side of your rib cage. When you start tapping this area, you move the energy in the liver. You begin to release the burden of angry feelings as well as the stress anger puts on your liver.

Now you're going to take it a few steps further.

You're going to:

1) release the illusion that somebody could actually hurt you,
2) embrace the fact that you are an amazing being who's learning new lessons,
3) acknowledge that you chose that teacher to teach you this lesson, and
4) accept the gift of this lesson by seeing the good that came out of a painful experience.

While you tap your liver, say, loud and clear, "I love and accept myself." Then take a breath. On the exhale, really feel the release. Our body only has so many ways to let go of stuff. We can sweat it out. We can pee or poop it out. Or we can just breathe it out.

So tap your liver and say, "I love and accept myself."
See how that feels. It's not something we say to
ourselves very often, let alone aloud. I want you to
say it out loud so ALL parts of you hear that.

Next, tap your liver and say, "I love and accept
myself, even if I'm having a hard time forgiving
_____ (fill in the blank) and releasing all this
anger. And I love and accept myself, when I now
choose to forgive myself and be at peace." Take
another deep breath.

Then say, "I love and accept myself when I now
choose to forgive and release joyfully." (Be sure to
emphasize "I NOW CHOOSE.") Take a final full, deep
breath and stop tapping.

The wording on this final statement is really important.
When you say, "I now choose," you are giving your
unconscious mind a command. That's what makes
this such an ingenious brain hack. The reason this
system works so beautifully is that it uses the limited
processing power of the conscious mind; you occupy
that part of your mind with tapping your liver. Because
you have to consciously focus on tapping and
speaking the words, your conscious mind is maxed
out. It cannot deal with more. It's similar to what
occurs in hypnosis. By giving the conscious mind
something to do, you can more readily get access to
the unconscious mind where the resources you need
reside. You're going in there and saying, "You know

what? It's okay if you feel angry. It's okay if you believe that you have a hard time forgiving. And I now choose to release that *anyway*."

True forgiveness is that moment when you decide, "I am no longer a victim of my past. I am no longer willing to give away my power to someone else. I'm claiming my freedom because I deserve to be happy."

I created my "Forgiveness Quickie" video as a guided exercise you can use to bring forgiveness into your heart and mind right when you need it most. Visit my digital resource guide to view the video and receive more clarity on how to use my "tapping" technique.

HAPPINESS TIP #4: Reframe Mistakes as "Interesting Ways of Learning."

When you catch yourself using your emotional energy to mull over some mistake, reframe the mistake as "an interesting way of learning." Then consciously redirect your emotional energy to bringing in more of what you want.

CHAPTER FOUR
Step 4: Own Your Desires

"Tired of trying to cram my sparkly star-shaped self into society's beige square holes, I choose to embrace my ridiculous awesomeness and shine like the freaking supernova I was meant to be."
~Unknown

In **Step 4, Own Your Own Desires**, we get into the *really* fun part where you get to create the life of your dreams. Let's do a quick review. So far, you've discovered that:

- Forbes magazine considers intuition the highest form of intelligence.
- Intuition is far more real than it's "woo-woo" reputation has led us to believe.
- Happiness and intuition go hand-in-hand.
- Intuition is viewed as a womanly attribute, but all people have it, regardless of where they fall on the gender spectrum.
- Intuition is a skill that can be developed just like any other skill.
- Establishing rapport with your unconscious mind will strengthen your intuition.
- You can access intuition more easily when in a relaxed brain state.
- Managing your emotions gives you greater access to your deep knowing.

After coaching thousands of people, including world-class athletes, politicians, managers, coaches, trainers and celebrities, I've identified the *internal shift* people make that puts their dreams within reach.

Become a Magnet for What You Truly Desire

You're about to go from a weak position to a powerful position, from "This is what I want" to "I'm staking my claim." This internal shift will supercharge your efforts and make you irresistible. The shift happens quite naturally when you *fully own your desire*.

Sounds simple, right? Not necessarily.

Truth be told, when you fully own your desire, you push up against a powerful taboo.

It may sound odd, but most of us have been conditioned to believe we can't have what we want. The conditioning goes even farther and tells us *it's not okay to want what we want*. This self-sabotage program hums along beneath our thoughts. We're barely aware of it, and we don't even hear the lyrics that go along with the hum.

Here is a sampling of some of those lyrical phrases:
- I don't even know what I want.
- You can't possibly ask for all that!
- What I want keeps changing.
- Nobody gets to have *that* much happiness.
- I can't have what I want, so why bother.
- I'll never succeed, nothing works for me…
- I don't deserve to have it all.
- I'll look like a fool if I fail.
- Who do you think you are, asking for so much?
- Shame on you for being so selfish!
- You're too big for your britches.
- Set goals that high and you're bound to be disappointed.
- People will think you're arrogant, cocky, GRANDIOSE!

Any of that sound familiar? It's pretty much the soundtrack for our culture.

Here's what I most want you to hear (and what the self-sabotage program doesn't want you to know), when you fully own what you want, you gain a huge advantage. You become a powerful magnet for all that you truly desire.

See, your heart's deepest longing has tremendous draw. The more you lean into that longing, the more your intuition will nudge you in the direction you need to go. The more you trust your intuitive knowing, the more wise counsel it will provide. Your natural gifts will begin to shine through in all that you do.

For that to happen, you need the "golden key" that opens the door to everything your heart desires… and more.

Align with Your Highest Destiny

So just what is the key that unlocks the door to your dreams? Is it the game plan and the tactics you use to get what you want in life? Do you need a better strategy to achieve the success you desire? Is it a matter of timing? A question of "not what you know but *who* you know"? Maybe you just need to find the right business partner or draft a business plan. Is motivation the all-important key?

The answer is yes… and no. All of the above can contribute to your success, but none of these factors will ensure that you succeed. What you need is a "No matter what" attitude and mindset.

As Tony Robbins points out, success is 80% psychology (mindset and attitude) and only 20% skills. Take a close look at any stuck situation in your life and notice how you're going about getting unstuck. For the most part, people focus on "the how" above all else. We fixate on the skills we need to develop, or obtaining the resources we need to get the job done. Meanwhile, we tend to overlook the crucial element to success. Oddly enough, this crucial element is the only part of the equation we truly CAN control, and that is the state of our mind. Any viable formula for success begins and ends with mindset and attitude.

Attitude is more important than all the strategy sessions in the world. Your mindset is more important than perfect timing, cunning tactics, an auspicious partnership, or a kick-butt business plan. Without a winning attitude, even investment capital doesn't guarantee success. Why? Because none of those external factors give you what you need most to succeed: the courage and resilience to face the obstacles. That can only come from inside. It's your attitude that gives you the drive you need to keep moving and not get stuck when you bump up against a setback or disappointment. A winning mindset can carry you through any failure or challenge. A positive attitude can even serve to buoy you up when others are doing their best to discourage you.

Attitude is more important than where you come from or any detail of your personal history. It's more important than your resumé or CV. It's more important than your education and talents. It even trumps intelligence. Attitude is what allows those people who don't seem to have "a head for business" to become extremely successful.

There's another big boon you get with a "No Matter What" attitude. It makes you immune to negativity. You can stand strong regardless of what other people think, say, or do. With a powerful attitude, you can remain neutral when the opinions of others are unfavorable. You can even stay clear-headed when their actions are meant to harm.

Taking this a little further, let's look at mindset. Your attitude is expressed in "where your head is at." Your mindset is your personal ethos; it's made up of the beliefs that drive what you think, say, and do. It's your mindset that determines whether you truly make your mark or settle for mediocrity.

Here's what is really beautiful about mindset and attitude: they can be learned. You develop a winning attitude with the everyday choices you make. Think of it like a dress code. You make a decision about what clothes you will wear every single day, right? Your attire and how you present yourself has a powerful impact on the impression you make on those you meet. The same is true of your attitude. So dress up in a positive attitude in the morning! I always start my day with a simple act of gratitude. Instead of getting out of bed with an "Oh, f!@#$" attitude, make it a habit to say "Thank you!" every single morning when you wake up. This simple practice has changed my life. Try it out!

Your history will no longer define you when you generate an attitude of infinite possibility. Set your sights on a beautiful future, and you align with your highest destiny. Bottom line: once you learn to maintain the mindset of possibility, that mindset becomes your secret weapon for success.

Claim Your Ground

In days gone by, pioneers would travel into unknown lands, stake a flag in the ground and say, "This is now MINE." That's what we do when we own our desires. We claim what is ours and become the champion of our heart's deepest longing.

To do that, most of us have to let go of guilt and shame. So many of us are blocked by our past in some way. We continue to carry this conditioned stigma that we are bad people. That guilt and shame is a very low frequency.

When we set out to live the life of our choosing, we evolve through levels of consciousness. This is how the soul evolves. The various levels of consciousness can actually be measured as distinct frequencies. Every emotion has its own frequency. For instance, love has a much higher frequency than anger. Anger has a higher frequency than guilt and shame. When we feel guilt and shame, we are running a frequency that is very close to depression. Depression is just under guilt and shame on the frequency scale.

89

STEP 4: Own Your Desires

Owning your desires is the quickest way to shift out of the frequency of guilt and shame.

The self-sabotage program no longer has power over you when you stake your claim by saying, "I am worthy. It's my destiny to fulfill my deepest desires." Say that again, and this time say it out loud: "I am worthy. It's my destiny to fulfill my deepest desires."

When you own that, you embrace the feeling of desire and recognize it for what it is—your heart's way of speaking to you. Your desire is your heart saying, "This would give me pleasure and make me feel joyful."

There are two parts to this step and both are accomplished with this declaration.

1) You empower yourself by giving your unconscious mind a super clear direction: *this is what I want.* Our default is to focus on the absence of what we desire. This declaration is a reset.
2) The natural result is that you start to focus on your desire. You've given your unconscious a new program to run. You start sending out positive thoughts that are directed toward your goal. That takes the effort out of manifesting what you want in life.

BRAIN HACK: Tap Your Courage Points

To supercharge your declaration "I am worthy" we developed this brain hack that incorporates your courage points.

Directly under your clavicle (aka, collar bones) are your courage points; they are also the end points of your kidney meridian. In Chinese medicine, your kidney meridian is associated with your adrenal glands, which produce adrenaline and cortisol, the hormones most closely linked with courage. Your adrenals quickly get stressed and depleted when we feel fear regardless of whether the perceived threat is real or imagined.

That brings us to why this brain hack works. When we don't own our desires, we tend to feel fearful. Our thoughts become muddy, "I don't know what I want… I can't possibly want *that*, it's way too way out there…" Muddy thoughts like these are quicksand for our desires. We slog around and essentially buy-in to fearful thoughts that stress our adrenals and kidneys. Left unchecked, we live in constant fear mode and readily go into burnout. And we can see from the happiness statistics where that takes us.

Tapping your courage points shifts you out of fear and into a more confident, courageous mode.

Tap your courage points and say, "I love and accept myself with all the fear that I'm feeling. And now I choose to release this fear and tap into my courage. I've got this. I can do this. I am brave."

This brings about a shift in your energy. You are training your brain to this more empowering thought rather than telling yourself what you can't do.

These are principles my husband Roy learned first as a world champion Martial Artist and later infused into his medical practice for over 35 years. He taught me the basic method in his outstanding Omega Healing Trainings and together we developed it further. You can learn more about this fast-working technique in his bestselling book, *Emotional Balance: The Path To Inner Peace and Healing* (Hay House, 2010; originally published in 1999 in the Netherlands under the title *Emotioneel Evenwhict*) and study Omega Healing as a multilingual online course (see more at www.mylife.it).

The Tangible Form of Grace

One thing we can all be sure of, life will throw us curveballs. With your new mindset, you won't have to duck and run. Be consistent in your application of these steps and your intuition will grow sure and strong. You'll be able to step into even the wildest curveball and knock it out of the park.

You'll start to trust your intuitive knowing more and more. In time, you will develop what I call *unshakable faith*. You'll simply know that you can handle whatever life serves up. In good times and bad, you will be accompanied by a deep sense of competence. You will stand on solid ground. This is grace in its most tangible form.

We often fear that if we fully own our desire we'll end up disappointed. Again, that's a default setting on a negative program. We hit the refresh button by getting really clear on what it is we truly want. There are times when what we want will change, of course. Life is never static. Fortunately, your intuition has its ear to the ground of your deep longing no matter how strong the winds of change.

One of the Most Difficult Decisions of My Life

It was time for to give up my business in Austria, cut links with Salzburg, Austria and move to Holland to be with Roy. My first thought was "What about the boys?" It didn't seem fair to ask them to give up their school and all their friends and move with me. And yet I of course wanted them to be with me. I wasn't sure how to handle it. My intuition told me to ask them what they would like to do. Jacob and George were 14 and 15 years of age. They were old enough to decide for themselves. I asked them what they thought, I encouraged them to speak from the heart and not hold back. "If you had all the choices in the world," I said, "what would you like to do? Would you like to come to Holland with me and Roy, or stay here with your Dad?"

They looked at each other, then back at me. The response was unequivocal. "We want to stay with Dad."

As hard as that was for me to hear, I understood. They wanted a chance to be with their dad, to have his undivided attention and love. The next step was to get him on board. He, too, was an immediate "Yes!"

I felt a bittersweet sadness. Yes, I would miss my boys. I couldn't even imagine what it would be like not to be with them day to day. At the same time I felt extremely grateful to have created an environment wherein they could own their desire and speak their truth.

They stayed with their dad for a year and a half. During that time, I flew to Salzburg every two weeks to see them and they came to visit me every few months. I missed being with them a lot and the constant travel was quite stressful, but I also knew they were happy, and this was the right thing to do.

When we started making plans to move to America, my intuition spoke loud and clear. The boys should come with us to the States; they needed to jump into this new adventure with me and Roy. No small challenge with two teenage boys who'd grown accustomed to living with their father and enjoying a high level of freedom and independence. But their grades had suffered. And I'd heard rumors of wild parties. It was time for them to be with their mom again. It was a lot to ask, but I spoke from my heart and shared my feelings. The boys agreed.

The first three months were difficult, especially for my younger son, George. But he adapted along with the rest of us and it was delightful to see how his self esteem blossomed with the challenge.

Today, both of my sons consider the decision to move to America one of the best they ever made. They now know what it's like to start fresh in a new country. It gave them the confidence that they can go anywhere and make their way.

It's so very tempting to focus on what we don't have and don't want. Whether it's the childhood friends we leave behind, the marriage that ends, or the business that fails, we shut down our intuition when we fixate on what we don't have. Looking out at life that way, we fail to see the vast possibilities that await us.

The shift you've made in Step 4, Own Your Desires, puts you in the ideal position to embrace that infinite potential and actively create the life you want. You've made the all-important internal shift from "I wish I could" to "I now choose to…" (complete the sentence with whatever will fulfill your wildest dreams).

POWER MOVE: Stand Your Ground

Strike a power pose. Stand with your feet shoulder width apart; make a fist with each hand and place your hands on your hips. Now say out loud: "I want what I want, and I'm worthy of it." Go ahead, say it again.

Psychologist Amy Cuddy popularized the notion of power poses in her popular TED Talk, "Your body language may shape who you are." Adopting this type of physical posture boosts feelings of confidence and can have a powerful positive impact on your mood. Research suggests it may very well impact your chances of success as well as your body chemistry.

HAPPINESS TIP #5: Take Off Your Shoes & Walk in the Grass

Take off your shoes and walk in the grass. Few are the simple things we can do as powerful as *grounding,* the practice of allowing your body to connect with the electromagnetic frequency of the Earth. The healing power of this energy field has meanwhile been proven many times over. If there is no grass available: Mentally imagine growing roots deep into the earth, allow them to dangle in the earth's core; use your breath to release all that no longer serves you and bring in all the healing electromagnetic frequencies from the Earth.

Now do this in conjunction with the Power Move above, Stand Your Ground. With your feet on the ground, say out loud: "I am safe and worthy of owning my desires. I deserve to be happy!" Say it three more times.

HAPPINESS TIP #6: Download & Listen to the Unshakeable Faith Audio

If you've read this far, you are beginning to feel what I mean by unshakeable faith. In the resource section you will find a link to download a free 20 minute audio called Unshakable Faith that will help you develop just that! Download it to your phone or tablet and let it play in the background while you do everyday tasks that don't require focused attention. Or put in your earbuds and take a 20 minute power nap while you listen. You can even go to sleep listening to this audio. It's a pep talk for your brain that will help you relax and know that everything's going to be okay. You will begin to sense, in a tangible way, that you have everything you need to accomplish your goal. With that kind of unshakable faith, you'll step up more often. You'll take more risks and more consistently hit the mark. Continue to own your desires and you'll find yourself standing up for them the way you might stand up for a child. You'll understand that your dreams are growing and need your loving care.

CHAPTER FIVE
Step 5: Tap Into the Universe

"My life seemed to be a series of events and accidents. Yet when I look back, I see a pattern."
— Benoît B. Mandelbrot

"Accidents happen. That's what everyone says. But in a quantum universe there are no such things as accidents, only possibilities and probabilities folded into existence by perception."
~ J. Michael Straczynski, *Before Watchmen: Nite Owl/Dr Manhattan*

In 1483, early explorers from Europe visit Haiti. They are amazed to see the natives playing with something they've never seen before: a ball that bounces! This marvelous invention is made out of tree sap, a milky substance the Haitians cure by smoking it with palm nuts.

Fast forward to 1736. A french astronomer returns from South America with a milky fluid the people of Peru use to make their shoes waterproof. Later that century, an English chemist notices that the same milky stuff can be used to rub out pencil marks. Thus, did the substance we know as "rubber" gets its name.

Fast forward another 100 years to the late 1830s. Inventor Joseph Goodyear is experimenting with rubber in his New England home. His wife and six children are out of the house and he has taken over the kitchen. He accidentally drops a mixture of rubber mixed with sulfur and white lead on the hot stove. But the mixture doesn't melt, it hardens to the consistency of tough leather. This leads to the invention of vulcanized rubber and earns Goodyear his first patent. Fifty years later, his blooper becomes the raw material for a new industry: automobile tires.

Accidents happen. All the time. What becomes of an accident depends entirely on those involved.

A Mess or a Masterpiece?

Benoît B. Mandelbrot was a Sterling Professor of Mathematical Sciences at Yale. He is credited with coining the word *fractal* to describe partly random or chaotic phenomena such as crystal growth, fluid turbulence, and galaxy formation. One of his pet theories looked at roughness and self-similarity in nature, the "uncontrolled element" in life. Take clouds or shorelines, for example. We might consider them messy and chaotic, nonetheless, they display a high degree of order. Mandelbrot called this "the art of roughness."

Life can often feel rough. Does it need to be like that? What if we could see it as a game that's designed to teach us incredible lessons and offer outstanding experiences? What if it's up to us to learn how to work with the Universe rather than against it?

This brings us to **Step 5, Tap Into the Universe**, one I am very passionate about teaching, especially in all four modules of my signature "Christallin Oracle Training: Tap Into the Universe." It is simultaneously the foundation and culmination of the other four steps because the moment you tap into your intuition, you open the channels to universal wisdom.

Take a quick look at human history and you will notice a simple truth: many of our greatest inventions were conceived in a moment of intuitive insight. Inventors have a knack for tapping into the wisdom of the universe and being able to see reality anew. Moments of intuitive insight that lead to new discoveries often occur after an "accident." Whether that accident is a catastrophe or mere inconvenience doesn't seem to matter. Intuition delivers many a marvel in response to human need.

We will put this marvelous responsiveness to work for you on a very personal level in Step Five. You will discover how easy it is to turn a seemingly unfortunate situation into a blessing. I've heard countless stories from people who've used **Step 5, Tap Into the Universe**, in stressful circumstances to create miraculous results.

Change is the Only Real Constant

Just as discussed in **Step 4, Own Your Desires**, mindset and attitude are of utmost importance when you want to Tap Into these. In this context, "Expect A Miracle" is far more than a cute bumper sticker. It's an attitude that sets up a field of positivity and makes miracles that much more likely to happen.

Combine a positive attitude with a mindset that says "anything is possible" and you send the universe a personalized invitation to bring on the miracles. In contrast, if you look at a situation as hopeless, the field around those circumstances shrinks. Once you label a situation "hopeless," you essentially tell your intuition, "There's no point, this is never going to change." You've just shut down your creativity.

Accidents happen. It's inevitable in our world. Same is true of inconveniences and natural disasters. It's the nature of existence. Whether a minor incident like a sticky spill or a disastrous event like a fireball in your living room, it's imperative to remember that change happens every second. Change is the only real constant in our lives. Moreover, we all have an innate ability to actually create change again and again. This tracks back to Step Four and taking ownership of our lives.

All the tools discussed so far encourage developing *behavioral adaptability,* which is the willingness to learn new ways to accomplish objectives and with a positive attitude. People who use these tools consistently find themselves feeling stuck and victimized far less often, if at all. Instead, they find themselves more and more in awe of the miracles all around us.

Littlewood's Law of Miracles

Over the course of his illustrious career, Cambridge University professor John Littlewood received six awards, including the Royal Medal, for his contributions to the field of mathematics. Outside his field, he is best known as the man who pulled the curtain on our belief that miracles are a supernatural phenomenon. Based on the general law of truly large numbers, he defined a miracle as an event with odds of one in a million. Littlewood's Law states that a person can expect a miracle about once a month. Not once in a lifetime or even once a year—once a month!

How would your life be different if you expected a big miracle once a month? Better yet, how would your life be different if you started looking around and appreciating the little miracles that happen every single day? A flower opens in the morning and you see a miracle. Your child smiles at you and you see a miracle. Whatever we appreciate increases over time. See miracles everywhere and you evoke miracle-thinking. Your mind expands, your horizons broaden, and your intuition bubbles with new possibilities at every turn.

Detained at Immigration Without My Husband

Roy and I were traveling back from Europe after teaching a sold-out workshop, of the Omega Healing Training in Italy. We'd had an audience of 700, including 500 people in the room and two hundred more joining us via livestream. We were equally exhausted and exhilarated.

We were keen to get back home as there'd been a minor snafu in our plans. My mom had come to watch the kids while we were away as usual, but she had to leave early on the day of our return. The boys, ages 16 and 17, would be taking care of our youngest, five year old Grace, until we got home late at night. It had been unusually cold in Asheville, and all the schools were closed due to heavy snow. That meant our kids would be stuck at home, alone, until we arrived.

After a 15 hour flight, we arrived on US soil and headed toward immigration. Roy went into the line for those with U.S. passports while I went into the longer line for those with foreign passports. I waited for the better part of an hour until it was my turn to step up to the counter.

The officer took his time clicking around on his computer before he looked up at me and asked, "Do you do something with hypnosis?"

I responded, "Yes, that's part of what I do."

He rang his buzzer and popped my passport into a yellow folder as I was whisked off to THE ROOM.

Until that moment, I'd only heard about the dreaded room. Once inside, another officer confiscated my phone and told me to wait. No explanation as to why, just, "Wait here."

After a brief moment of panicky feelings, I realized that I would not be able to figure out this one out with my conscious mind and took a deep breath. I would have to trust my intuition to navigate the situation.

For over two hours, I waited in what appeared to be an interrogation room. I had no water and no clue why I'd been detained.

I used all of my tools to avoid freaking out as fearsome thoughts raced through my brain: "My kids are alone at home… what if they send me back to Europe… what will I do if I can't go home?" My mind dropped in on a scene I'd actually witnessed wherein a woman got led away in handcuffs and put back on a plane. I thought of our nanny who'd just recently been denied entry to the States for no good reason even though she had a valid ESTA. You can imagine the frenzy going on inside me.

I did what I know to be the best strategy in times of crisis: pray and meditate. I touched base with my intuition and heard: "Keep calm. Breathe. Stay positive. This is all going to be just perfect."

"Pfffft," said my rational mind. "That's easier said than done when you know your kids are home, you can't contact your husband and, you've missed your connection home. What could possibly be perfect here?"

I took command of my thoughts by using the tools you have learned in this book and making endless gratitude lists in my mind. After two hours of waiting, the officer returned. He handed me my belongings and said, "You're free to go now."

"That's it?" I muttered under my breath as I exhaled a sigh of relief that must've been audible in Africa. "Now to find Roy…"

After we hugged like long-lost friends, we were able to get re-booked on the last flight to Asheville. It was all going to be okay after all. We'd be home by midnight.

But it was not to be. We boarded the plane and were settling into our seats when the pilot announced that we would not be taking off due to snow and strong winds. We would have to spend the night in Atlanta and fly on the next day.

My heart plummeted. I was tired and frustrated; I just wanted to get home to my kids. We arrived at the hotel and called the kids. They were very grown up about it all. (Actually they were the ones comforting us…) I went to bed trusting it was all for the best and feeling grateful I could finally get some sleep.

Safe and sound in Asheville the next day, we had a happy reunion with the kids. Late that afternoon I realized just how much good had come of this "unfortunate" circumstance. There'd been a big accident on the highway in Asheville the night before. Had we returned on our original schedule, we could have been involved. Even if we weren't directly involved, we certainly would have been caught up in the traffic backup. Had the Universe spared us by "arranging" the delay at immigration?

There was another surprising benefit to the "senseless" delay. I never would have left my three kids alone overnight in a snowstorm, and yet they had managed beautifully. I saw a new kind of happy in their faces. They were proud of how they'd handled it, and they were closer for having looked after each other. Our unfortunate circumstance had forged a deeper bond between the three of them.

Once again, I was reminded, Trust Your Intuition!

The Happy Accident

These examples are a small sample of the remarkable outcomes we can expect when we're tapped into the universe. We often stumble into universal wisdom when we're in a crunch or faced with a crisis. What if we could intentionally tap into that vast knowing without the pressure of some kind of threat? What might we discover if we were to invite happy accidents to show us improved ways of getting things done?

Whether it's a personal crunch like getting detained by authorities, a brand new product like rubber, or an a emergency situation like a natural disaster, when we're tapped into the universe, great innovations and adaptations result. For that to happen more often, we need to be able to enter a relaxed brain state.

How do you enter a relaxed brain state when you're in stressful circumstances?

In a world full of chaos and messiness, how do you turn the "roughness" into art?

What miracles might occur if you embrace the inconveniences life throws your way?

How would you deal with life's inevitable rough patches if you had complete faith that some good fortune would come of it?

Later in this chapter, I'll will teach you the Christallin Command, a simple technique that allows you to turnaround even the toughest challenge. Use this method and you can actually prove the veracity of IIQ, both to yourself and to those around you. This supercharged command blends several fun brain hacks into one. It is used by thousands of people around the world who have taken our courses, such as the hundreds of Omega Healing Coaches and Christallin Oracles. I get letters all the time that testify to the power of this command to unleash our highest form of intelligence.

Before I teach you the command, I want to explore the three distinct brains in the human body: the heart brain, the head brain, and the gut brain (see the Resource section for more). We use all three brains when we make decisions and take action. Unfortunately, when people don't know the best way to use their three brains, they often make decisions on the basis of fear and greed.

Discernment - When Does Your Heart Say "Yes"?

The wise way to use these three brains is to go to the heart first because the heart is always the leader. One of the biggest mistakes we make is letting the head brain lead. As Tony Robbins says, "If you're in your head, you're dead." As we've seen, the conscious mind has extreme limitations. Relying too heavily on what we can "think our way through" often keeps us trapped. We can escape that trap by allowing the heart to be the leader of our lives. We do that by going into the heart first and asking for direction. Your heart will always make loving choices. Your heart is always aligned with our highest intention. Your heart knows what is in the highest good in tough situations. The heart can see its way clear to the most compassionate choice. Your heart knows the kindest thing to say. "What would love do?" That is the question your heart always asks.

When we know what direction we're headed in, and our heart has said yes to that goal, we go up to our brain and ask for the how.

How do you know when the heart says yes? There are many ways your heart can signal yes. All of them feel good. Sometimes you know your heart is a "Yes!" simply because you feel happy. Sometimes, your heart feels kind of excited. Sometimes your heart will start singing.

Your heart is especially adept at leading when you're faced with tough decisions that might have negative consequences. If you follow your heart, it might upset someone (but then again you always run that risk... because there is no way you can please everybody, right?) . Nonetheless, you have to make a decision. To follow your heart-knowing in that moment may make you even feel momentarily unhappy. Some heartfelt decisions actually make us sad because we know it will involve change and possibly letting go of something or someone.. Nonetheless, if you follow the heart's prompting in difficult circumstances, you'll feel a softening and opening inside. It's as if your heart and mind are getting together and saying, "Yes, that feels right."

Tune into your heart's knowing on a regular basis and you'll start to hear your heart sing. The songs it sings will be unique to the situation, but the voice will be clear and strong.

This is an important key to tapping into the universe: developing discernment. The voice of the heart is not a booming voice. It's a subtle voice, a voice we must train ourselves to hear. Tune in the next time you are faced with a difficult choice. Learn to hear the difference. If the voice is coming from fear or lack, if it is colored with self-doubt and self-judgment, you are hearing the voice of the small self. Fearful voices are a conglomerate with a negative vibration. The heart speaks softly; it's vibratory quality is always uplifting. The heart sees the higher good and the greater meaning behind what's happening, even in the presence of suffering or anger.

The One Thing you Need to Do

Once the heart is aligned with the direction you are going and you have that yes, then you go up to the head brain and ask for the how. It's the head brain's job to come up with a strategy; it loves to figure out the "how." The head brain knows how to get where you're going. It can see the action steps that lead to the goal. The head brain is good at linear, sequential, spatial calculations. Your heart sees the vision and holds the goal, your head is the master planner.

Once those action steps have been identified, go back to the heart and say, "Okay. Are these action steps the right ones to take?"

Obviously, one could get wildly creative and go through iteration after iteration on the action steps they might take given unlimited time to ponder on those strategies. That's when it's helpful to go back to Step 1, Get Out of the Buzz, again. Remember, the 5 steps build on each other.

Once your heart gives you a "yes" on the strategies your brain has come up with, you turn to your gut. The brain in your gut supplies the grit. You ask your gut for the courage to take the necessary action to achieve your goals.

If we want to enjoy success, we need to honor the principles of success. One of the primary principles of success is taking action. The formula for success is simple. Have a clear goal. Be very specific about that goal. Take consistent action steps towards that goal.

Learn to use the three brains wisely as described above and you'll begin making wiser choices. The road to success becomes smoother because you're not battling the limitations that arise when you use your gut brain to do what your head brain can do better. It's so easy to get lost in your head trying to "figure it out." Meanwhile, your heart often knows the ONE thing you need to do to get you closer to your goal. Focus on that ONE highest priority and watch yourself move ahead far more gracefully.

Another pitfall we often fall into is getting side-tracked when trying to juggle too many projects and to-dos at the same time. We need to remember what we learnt in kindergarten: one step at a time! Focus on the ONE thing that is highest priority and get that done first. Similarly, we often get stuck looking for answers when what we really need is the courage to act.

In all of these situations, the following simple brain hack can bring you back into your heart and optimize your ability to Tap Into the Universe. You will find many more ideas on how to develop the relentless courage to act on your heart's desires and follow your intuition in the resource section.

BRAIN HACK: Deep Belly Breathing

The easiest way to get those three brains to work in the correct sequence and access the power of your heart is to close your eyes and focus on your breath.

Take three to five minutes; that's all you need. Set your timer or turn on a meditation track and do five-count breathing. Simply count to five while you breathe in, then count to five while you breath out. As you do this five-count breathing, call to mind an image of someone you love, or something really beautiful such as a bunch of flowers or favorite place in nature. Your heart will become entrained to that beauty and start beating in a very harmonious way. You will evoke the state of compassion.

The HeartMath Institute has done a great deal of research that demonstrates the power of this type of entrainment. But you don't need to be a research scientist to prove to yourself the power of deep breathing. You will immediately feel the change in your breath as it goes from very shallow chest breathing using only about a third of the breathing apparatus, to full deep belly breaths that involve more of your lungs and diaphragm.

Five-part breathing is an effective way to reduce anxiety and an excellent way to enter into deep sleep. It is also one of the simplest ways to tune into your intuition and tap into the vast wisdom of the universe. You can do it anytime, anywhere.

STEP 5: Tap Into the Universe

We've talked a lot about tapping into the Universe. The question remains, how do you do that in the midst of the wild ride of life?

First and foremost, you need an effective way to access your intuition and THE healing brainwave state. Neuroscience tells us that theta brainwaves are our most healing of the brainwaves. So how do we get our brains into theta? In general, we enter the theta brainwave state during deep sleep when we're unconscious. We can also get into theta during meditation. However, it may take years of practice before we can readily get into theta and stay awake. Ordinary states of consciousness are characterized by beta brainwaves.

The Christallin Command is a super-charged brainwave hack that enables anyone to go into theta within seconds AND state a crystal clear intention. That's an incredibly powerful skill to have and one that will vastly increase your ability to Tap Into the Universe and develop your IIQ.

The Christallin Command

This ingenious brain hack combines many different modalities. Its benefits will be obvious from the very first time you use it. A perfect way to get into the ideal state for setting crystal-clear intentions and goals, it also works absolutely beautifully when you have no clue what to do.

First you'll use eye movements to get into theta.

Start by taking a few deep breaths and close your eyes. Become aware of your grounding. Imagine you have roots growing out of the soles of your feet or simply take a few deep breaths and connect with the earth beneath you. Be 100% present for a moment.

Now roll your eyes upwards as if you're looking through the crown of your head. This shifts you into theta.

Keep your eyes rolled upwards and say this incantation/programming command (preferably out loud): "Even if I don't know how..."

Complete the sentence with whatever it is you don't know how to do in the moment, for example: "Even if I don't know how to relax. Even if I don't know how to make peace. Even if I don't know how to speak my truth. Even if I don't know to release this anger."

Then take a deep breath and, keeping your eyes rolled up, say: "All I do know is that it is so now."

In this part of the programming sentence you're letting your conscious mind off the hook for not knowing

115

how. That's an important step because the number one question the conscious mind keeps asking is: "How? How? How?" It gets stuck there because we don't know, and often can't know the "how" at a conscious level.

This tracks back to what Einstein said about the mind that created the problem is not the mind that will find the solutions. We have to tap into our intuition, into the greater mind, to find solutions to our problems.

By saying this to our conscious mind, we help it relax. We're admitting that we don't know how and, at the same time, we declare what we do know: that it is so now. That's the first part of the command.

Then, keeping your eyes rolled upward, you say: "I delete, delete, delete all programming within me that is stopping me from achieving this goal or sabotaging me."

Follow that up with: "And I download, download, download all the resources I need to achieve this goal now effortlessly, gracefully, joyfully."

Finish with gratitude by saying: "Thank you. Thank you. Thank you."

Again, the Christallin Command involves many fun brain hacks in one powerful command.

Here's the sequence:
1) Get your brain into theta.
2) Give your brain a super clear command.
3) Delete any programming that is not beneficial to you or your system.
4) Bring in, download, and program your brain with whatever you need to succeed.
5) Specify how you're going to succeed: with grace, ease and joy.

This final piece is important because we need to be very specific with the unconscious mind. We're not giving a command to succeed at any cost regardless of the price or hard work involved. We're saying we choose to succeed with grace, ease and joy. When we add those three components, we give a specific command as to how we choose to manifest. We're not coming from force. Rather, we're coming from a state of unshakable faith.

The last part is also very important, saying thank you three times. That taps into gratitude. When we feel gratitude, it's impossible to feel anger or worry. Gratitude is the frequency that is the most powerful for manifestation. When we come from a state of "I have, and I feel grateful for what I have," the universe will give us more of that.

HAPPINESS TIP #7: Take a Dance Break

Take a dance break.

The simple act of stopping what your doing, turning on your favorite music and dancing around the room can transmute any energetic blockage or mood state into a turn on. You can turn any situation around 180 degrees simply by breaking the trance of whatever is happening and shifting into a state of love and joy. As you dance, ask yourself the question: "What is the blessing here?" Love is the highest vibration in the universe; it has tremendous transformative power. We can make a choice to shift out of a negative state by tapping into love.. This can even work when you're in physical pain. Start by acknowledging what's so and shift the energy by saying, "Obviously, I'm in pain right now. How do I find the pleasure?" Engage with your entire body and mind as you dance.

Set a clear intention: "With this simple act of turning on the music I invite my brain to snap out of it and transmute this pain into pleasure." Then start moving, and asking the question "Where's the pleasure here?"

HAPPINESS TIP #8: Say "Yes!" a Hundred Times a Day

Set yourself the goal to say "Yes!" a hundred times a day.

For example, my daughter and I have a ritual we do when we drive to school in the morning. We play one of her favorite songs and sing "Yes" to the song the entire time. It feels absolutely incredible!

The energy that happens within us when we say "Yes!" is so uplifting we can actually create a vortex of manifestation. I think of it as a blueprint of positivity. This is absolutely essential because how we feel in the present moment determines how we experience our world and what we're manifesting in our future. Every single thought we think is heard by every single cell in our body. Those thoughts go out like radio waves. We're actually transmitting the energy of our thoughts out into the universe. You can see this in action when you sing-along with your favorite song. Try singing "Yes" for just a few lines and see what happens.

CONCLUSION
Where Do We Go From Here | My Call to Urgency

Intuition tells me, if you've read this far, you are one of the people Pulitzer Prize winner Alice Walker was referring to in the title of her New York Times Bestseller, *We Are the Ones We've Been Waiting For: Inner Light in a Time of Darkness.*

I've written this book for "the ones" who are really brave and ready to take a giant step toward a better future. Difficult times require us to move beyond conventional ways of looking at life. We need a more effective way to process information so we can step into this new way of seeing. When we see with new eyes, we develop new ways of being with ourselves and with each other.

At this point in human history, we cannot afford to look away from the stark realities; we must look at them head-on. We have to take stock of where we are in order to get clear where we're going. Even those of us who place a high value on positive thinking can see the writing on the walls. The statistics are alarming, and if expert predictions are correct, our situation will continue to get worse unless a major shift in consciousness occurs. The World Health Organization predicts that within the next 10 years, depression and suicide will be the #1 cause of death on a global scale. This is a horrific prognosis that has the potential to put a massive economic and sociological burden on our societies.

I saw this in China while teaching there in 2011, and the situation continues to worsen. I was deeply shocked to learn that young people, even children, struggle with severe depression. Did you know that Chinese universities require parents to sign a release waiver so the university cannot be sued if the child commits suicide? Some universities have actually put nets on the roofs of tall buildings to prevent students from jumping off.

We need to create a dramatic shift. We need to see this challenge as an opportunity and responsibility. I believe the best place to begin is to develop our intuition. It is the "trim-tab" that will turn us in a new direction.

One of the great intuitive geniuses of the 20th century, Buckminster "Bucky" Fuller, was fond of the trim tab metaphor as a way to understand personal responsibility and the power or choice. Deeply depressed after his daughter's death, Bucky fell into a deep depression. Thirty-two at the time, he went alone into the ocean and swam far away from shore in an attempt to put an end to it all. It was a marker moment in his life. From within a desperate state of mind, an all-knowing awareness delivered the insight that he hadn't really given his life a chance. Questions arose in his mind: Who am I to waste a life? Is life really worth living? He decided to turn his life into an experiment and decided to find out what a single human life could achieve. His achievements speak for themselves.

When we tune into what we need to be happy and trust our highest intelligence, we can begin to work with the Universe to make rapid change happen. In my mind, the big question at this moment in history is: what are we going to leave behind? **What are we leaving for our children? Will we leave them a mess to clean up, or will we leave them a masterpiece to be admired?**

You have the power within you to shape your world. Use these 5 Steps, Happiness Tips, Power Moves to fully embrace that power and you will develop unshakable faith. Then you will come to realize that you have all the resources you need to turn the world on its head and make your life and the lives of those around you a masterpiece.

Please use my **Online Resource Guide** to continue your journey from here. Unlock your resources using the code 444. Access the guide here: https://joymartina.com/joys-resources/

Be Well,
Joy Martina

JoyMartina.com
Published July 2018

Printed in Great Britain
by Amazon